(Ire) Bayakoa (Arg) Beautiful Pleasure Black Tie Affair (Ire) Boston Harbor Brave Raj Brocco Buck's Boy

iana Cozzene Da Hoss Dance Smartly Dancing Spree Daylami (Ire) Desert Stormer

S0-BNS-972

and Gulch Hollywood Wildcat In the Wings (GB) Inside Information Is It True Jewel Princess Kotashaan (Fr)

sque Miss Alleged Northern Spur (Ire) One Dreamer Open Mind Opening Verse Outstandingly Paseana (Arg)

ud Truth Reraise Rhythm Ridgewood Pearl (GB) Royal Academy Royal Heroine (Ire) Sacahuista Safely Kept

n (GB) Storm Song Success Express Sunday Silence Tasso Theatrical (Ire) Thirty Slews Tikkanen Timber

Answer Lively A.P. Indy Arazi Arcangues Artax Awesome Again Barathea (Ire) Bayakoa (Arg) Beautiful

hief Cherokee Run Chief Bearhart Chief's Crown Cigar Concern Countess Diana Cozzene Da Hoss Dance

nd Flanders Fly So Free Fraise Gilded Time Great Communicator Go for Wand Gulch Hollywood Wildcat In

n (Ire) Life's Magic Lit de Justice Lure My Flag Manila Meadow Star Miesque Miss Alleged Northern Spur

e Chatter Pilsudski (Ire) Pleasant Stage Precisionist Princess Rooney Prized Proud Truth Reraise Rhythm

Silverbulletday Skip Away Skywalker Smile Soaring Softly Spinning World Steinlen (GB) Storm Song Success

bridled's Song Very Subtle Wild Again Ajina Alphabet Soup Alysheba Anees Answer Lively A.P. Indy Arazi

arbor Brave Raj Brocco Buck's Boy Capote Cardmania Cash Run Cat Thief Cherokee Run Chief Bearhart

sert Stormer Eillo Eliza Elmhurst Epitome Escena Favorite Trick Ferdinand Flanders Fly So Free Fraise

True Jewel Princess Kotashaan (Fr) Lady's Secret Lashkari (GB) Last Tycoon (Ire) Life's Magic Lit de Justice

Verse Outstandingly Paseana (Arg) Pebbles (GB) Personal Ensign Phone Chatter Pilsudski (Ire) Pleasant Stage

roine (Ire) Sacahuista Safely Kept Sheikh Albadou (GB) Silic (Fr) Silverbulletday Skip Away Skywalker Smile

Thirty Slews Tikkanen Timber Country Twilight Ridge Unbridled Unbridled's Song Very Subtle Wild Again

This is the sound that brings the world's greatest horses, trainers, and jockeys together for an afternoon of world-class racing on Breeders' Cup Championship day.

SILIC (Fr) - 1999 Mile

Silic was raced sparingly throughout 1999, as trainer Julio Canani tried to keep him fresh for the Breeders' Cup Mile at Gulfstream Park. The strategy worked. Silic was ready for the race of his life. Under a well-judged ride from Corey Nakatani, one of the nation's premier jockeys in grass races, Silic (far left, number 12) rallied boldly to win a thriller for owners Terry Lanni, Bernie Schiappa and Ken Poslosky.

BREEDERS' CUP

THOROUGHBRED RACING'S CHAMPIONSHIP DAY

BY JAY PRIVMAN

FOREWORD BY BILL SHOEMAKER

Breeders' Cup: Thoroughbred Racing's Championship Day
© 2000 by Breeders' Cup Limited and Moonlight Press
All Rights Reserved.

ISBN 1-57243-413-9
Library of Congress Card Number 00-103820

No part of this book may be reproduced by any means,
including but not limited to photocopying, photographing,
scanning or electronic or mechanical means of data storage,
reproduction or retrieval without the prior written
permission of the copyright holders.

Printed in Hong Kong

Triumph Books
601 South LaSalle Street
Chicago, Illinois 60605
(312) 939-3330
Fax (312) 663-3557

Executive Editor: Leonard Lusky
Mechanical Production: Regency Books
Advertising: Power Graphics
Developmental Consultant: Bill Doolittle
Webmaster: Sherry Sherry
Administrative Assistant: Whitney Dickerson
Breeders' Cup Managing Editor: Damon Thayer
Breeders' Cup Project Manager: Peggy Gdovka
Breeders' Cup Art Director: Kathy Heitz
Breeders' Cup Proofreader: Carol Paulick

Moonlight Press would also like to thank Richard Jones, Shari House,
McKay Smith and Carl Nafzger.

Breeders' Cup®, Breeders' Cup Championship®, and the Official
Breeders' Cup logo are registered marks in the United States and may
not be used without the express written
permission of Breeders' Cup Limited.

*Previous page: Reraise played catch me if you can, and no one
could. He set wicked fractions in the 1998 Breeders' Cup Sprint at
Churchill Downs and kept right on rolling to make his trainer, 27-
year-old Craig Dollase, the youngest to win a Breeders' Cup race.
It was a family affair. Dollase's brother-in-law, Corey Nakatani,
rode Reraise, who was owned by a partnership of Dollase, Barry
Fey, Moon Han, and Frank Sinatra.*

ACKNOWLEDGMENTS

A project like this requires the concerted efforts of a
number of people behind the scenes. First and foremost is
Leonard Lusky of Moonlight Press, who conceptualized the idea,
brought me together with the Breeders' Cup, kept the project
rolling along, and saw it through to completion. The Breeders'
Cup staff, particularly Peggy Gdovka and Kathy Heitz, spent
countless hours poring over and fine tuning the content and lay-
out. This book looks as good as it does because of them.

Having covered a number of sports as a journalist, one
of the alluring aspects of racing is that most participants are
unfailingly cooperative, which is not the case in most of the
sporting world. Those who were interviewed for this book, including the legendary Bill Shoemaker, who shared his thoughts
for the Foreword, were eager to have their stories told, and their
enthusiasm and graciousness were invaluable.

This book is dedicated to my family—Joan, Irving,
Susan, Adam, and Ariel—who now understand why I much
preferred to have my nose in the Racing Form instead of my
biology book when I was in school. I would like to thank the
great horses who have competed through the years in the
Breeders' Cup—especially my personal favorite, Sunday
Silence—because it is their stories that made this book possible.

And I would also like to remind you that not every
horse ends up a Breeders' Cup champion, so please support the
retirement organizations that care for the animals who bring us
so much pleasure.

—*Jay Privman*

On behalf of Breeders' Cup Limited it is my pleasant
duty to acknowledge the many enthusiastic men and women
without whose efforts the racing history so beautifully profiled in
this book would not exist.

We wish to give special thanks to all of our stallion and
foal nominators through the years whose faith and support made
the Breeders' Cup a reality; to our officers, directors and founding members whose leadership, past and present, has so successfully guided the program; to each and every member of our staff
and agencies whose professionalism and energy have breathed
daily life into the corporation; to the members of the media and
our network partner NBC Sports for their artful coverage and
belief in racing's championship; to our host tracks and host com-
munities for their hospitality and partnership; to the international legion of racing fans, the most loyal and passionate group
in all of sports; to the owners, jockeys, trainers and their staffs
for their skill and perseverance; and finally to the magnificent
equine athletes whose displays of speed and courage have in-
spired millions.

—*D.G. Van Clief, Jr.*

Favorite Trick (number 3) bursts from the starting gate in the 1997 Breeders' Cup Juvenile at Hollywood Park. A little more than 100 seconds later, he had crossed the wire first, completing a perfect, 8-for-8 season, and securing the title of Horse of the Year. He became only the second 2-year-old to win the Eclipse Award as Horse of the Year, following the great Secretariat in 1972.

Table of Contents

Foreword

by Bill Shoemaker

When I came on the racing scene in California in 1949, horse racing was popular from coast to coast. There were important races in the East and West, and every summer we rode in Chicago, where there were big-money stakes with lots of prestige.

In those days, famous sportswriters covered the Kentucky Derby, Preakness, and Belmont Stakes, and the Triple Crown really spotlighted horse racing. Swaps and Nashua was a great rivalry of the 1950s, like Affirmed and Alydar in the 1970s. Such stars as Secretariat, Seattle Slew, and Spectacular Bid captured the public's imagination. Avid fans followed racing all year and became especially attached to the older handicap stars like Kelso, Forego and Native Diver, who battled season after season.

But over time, horse racing found itself in a battle with other sports for attention. It seemed like the only racing event that really mattered to sports fans was the Kentucky Derby. On the first Saturday in May, all eyes turned to Churchill Downs. But what happened the rest of the year in racing kind of lost out to baseball, football, basketball, and all the new participation sports like golf and tennis.

What horse racing needed was a big, new idea that would refocus attention on the horses and people who make this game so compelling.

Fortunately, there always has been someone in racing who could envision a new idea and work to see that it became a reality. Long ago, Col. Meriwether Lewis Clark and Col. Matt Winn dreamed big thoughts for the Kentucky Derby and saw those dreams come true. In the 1940s and 1950s, Warren Wright developed Calumet Farm into a racing powerhouse and a nostalgic legend.

But by the 1980s racing needed something big to revitalize the sport, and it got it when John Gaines stepped up with a new dream for Thoroughbred racing that became the Breeders' Cup.

Mr. Gaines' idea was to create a day of million-dollar championship races at the end of the racing season that would highlight all the kinds of horses that make our sport so interesting—2-year-olds, turf horses, fillies, and older stakes stars—not just the 3-year-olds who run in the Derby.

He also saw the potential of including foreign horses in the Breeders' Cup races, with the stars from overseas flying in to give the day an international flavor. That's been a great success, from the brilliant triumphs of horses like Arazi, Miesque and Daylami, to the fans getting closer in the paddock to see the dashing way the Europeans trim the manes and tails of their runners. The Breeders' Cup also spotlights the people of many countries, with stars as diverse as my friend Laffit Pincay, Jr. and England's great Lester Piggott competing over the same stretch of ground for million-dollar purses. I can tell you that riding against the greats from overseas was a real thrill for me. And I know my old pals Eddie Arcaro and Johnny Longden would have loved riding in a Breeders' Cup with all those bragging rights at stake, not to mention the big purses.

The entire affair was eventually called the Breeders' Cup, which is a perfect name because it describes the whole cycle of horse racing. The process begins with the breeding of Thoroughbred babies. Those babies grow up to be racehorses, and the cycle continues through their racing careers to the day when the stars of the track return

Bill Shoemaker following his win aboard Ferdinand in the 1987 Breeders' Cup Classic.

to the farms to father and mother a new generation of Thoroughbreds to venture out on conquests of their own. Our sport is unique in that way. It's a cycle that is complete and continuing. Now that the Breeders' Cup has been in existence nearly two decades, we find the stars of each season often trace to stars of past Breeders' Cups.

A good example of that is Strawberry Road, a horse I rode in the very first Breeders' Cup Turf in 1984. Strawberry Road was born in Australia, his sire Whiskey Road was born in France, his grandsire Nijinsky was born in Kentucky, and his great-grandsire Northern Dancer was born in Canada. That's a pretty worldly pedigree.

Strawberry Road ran fourth and second in two Breeders' Cup tries, then was retired to stallion duty at Allen Paulson's Brookside Farm in Kentucky, where he has sired three horses who have won Breeders' Cup races: Ajina, Escena, and Fraise. That continuity enriches the sport and provides fans with a long-range perspective of what horse racing is all about.

Television has been wonderful in telling that story, and is probably the most important factor in the success of the Breeders' Cup. NBC's coverage spans 4 1/2 hours of prime Saturday afternoon time in the fall, bringing horse racing to millions of mainstream and casual sports fans.

I had the honor of riding in 14 Breeders' Cup races, and even had a Breeders' Cup starter as a trainer. But the highlight for me was the famous Breeders' Cup Classic of 1987. Not only was there a $3 million purse on the line, but the field was packed with terrific racing stars—including two Kentucky Derby winners, Ferdinand and Alysheba.

Two of the sport's most famous trainers saddled the Derby winners in that Classic, with Charlie Whittingham sending out Ferdinand, and Jack Van Berg saddling Alysheba. Charlie had me on Ferdinand and Jack had Chris McCarron in the irons on Alysheba. Both Chris and I knew we were sitting on dynamite that day.

On the Wednesday before the race I worked Ferdinand five furlongs for Charlie in :57 4/5, which was the same kind of sharp workout the horse had before the Derby the year before. Ferdinand was still a kind of lazy horse, but that work got his mind on business, and I was able to keep him closer to the pace in the race.

I didn't want Ferdinand to make the lead too soon because he had a tendency to relax when he got in front. But I was kind of worried nearing the sixteenth pole as to whether I was going to get by Judge Angelucci, so I had to get him going. I saw Alysheba coming up on the outside and I just waited and waited. Then I shook the stick at Ferdinand and let him go to the lead. He saw Alysheba coming in just enough time to put forth a little extra effort right at the finish.

At the wire it was so close, neither Chris nor I knew who won. It was the same for the fans in the stands, and for millions of people watching on television. "The two Derby winners hit the wire together!" shouted NBC announcer Tom Durkin. While we were pulling up around the turn after the race, the TV broadcasters replayed the finish. And replayed it again in slow motion because you still couldn't tell.

It was finally settled by the photo finish camera, which showed Ferdinand winning by the slimmest of noses. I know when we turned our horses and came back to the stands, Chris and I were both physically and emotionally drained. And so were Ferdinand and Alysheba. They'd given it everything.

The next year Chris won the Breeders' Cup Classic on Alysheba at Churchill Downs, and he's won six other Breeders' Cup races. But, I know for me, Ferdinand winning that Classic was the thrill of a lifetime. And a thrill for millions of old, and new, racing fans.

Which is what the Breeders' Cup is all about.

—May 2000

A jockey makes 10 percent of the winner's share, meaning the winning jockey in the Breeders' Cup Classic earns more than $200,000. With prize money like that on the line, no wonder jockeys step lively when heading to the paddock.

I. History

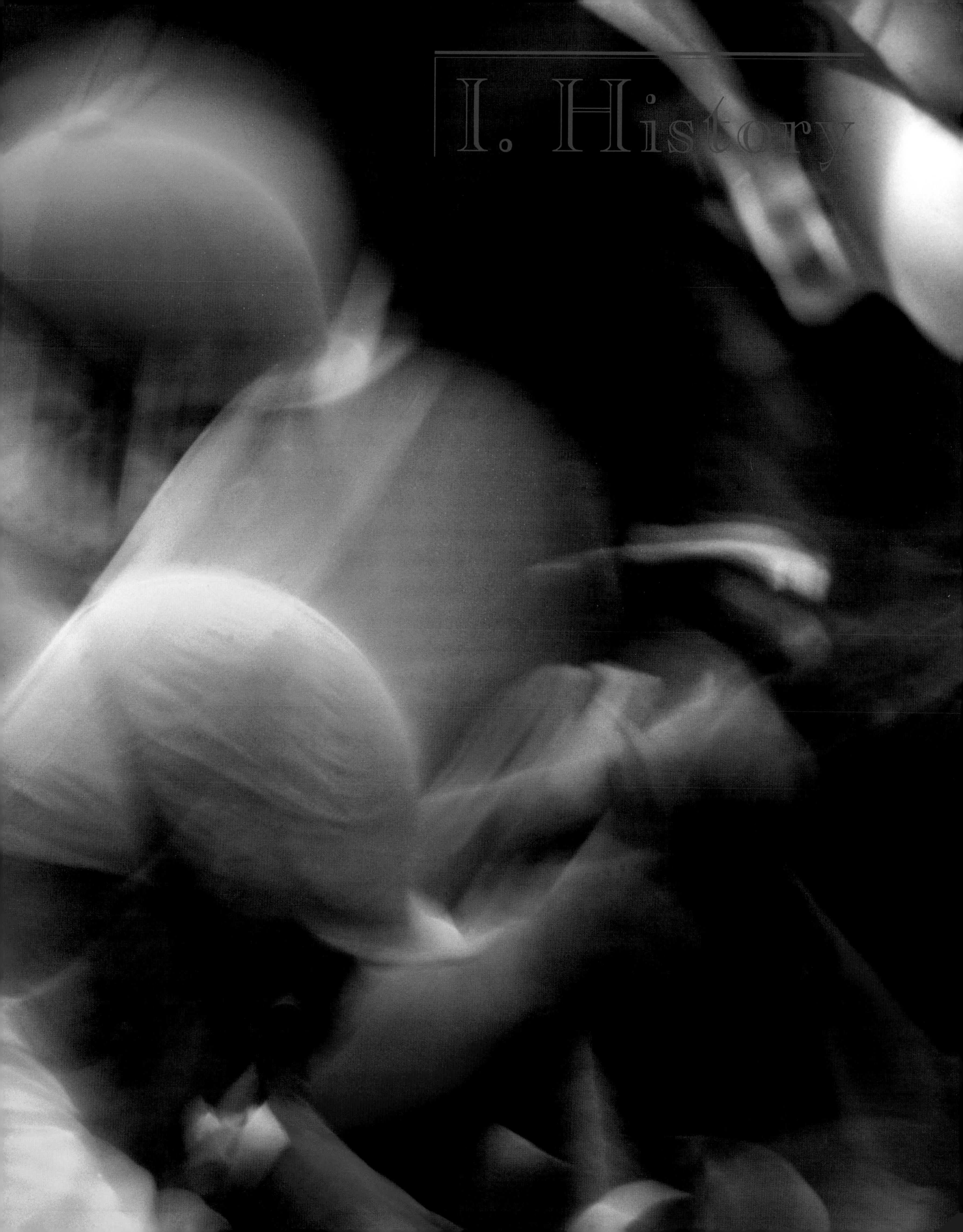

John Gaines had formed the idea in his mind. But he needed support. Thoroughbred racing, as he saw it, too often was blinded by self-interest. Never before had the disparate interests in the sport been joined for the good at the level he was intent on proposing. He needed owners, trainers, and racetracks to come together for a common goal. But first he needed help from his fellow breeders.

Gaines, who owned Gainesway Farm in Lexington, Kentucky, had an audacious plan. Spurred into action in the early 1980s after watching a nationally televised show that painted racing as being a haven for drug use, Gaines sought to counteract that image with a televised day of racing unlike no other. He envisioned championship races for horses in several divisions, each race worth at least $1 million, all on one afternoon, all on network television. It would take place in the fall, and serve to determine the sport's champions.

Knowing his plan would meet resistance and skepticism, Gaines sought to take several close friends into his counsel before going public. One of the first persons he approached was John Galbreath, who owned Darby Dan Farm.

Galbreath lived in Columbus, Ohio, so Gaines flew up there one afternoon. He briefly outlined his plan, then asked Galbreath his opinion.

"You must be smoking pot," Galbreath said.

Undaunted, Gaines continued with his presentation, taking the outline and enriching each point with detail as to how the project would work. Gaines desperately needed breeders like Galbreath to support him. He believed their financial backing would be the backbone of and catalyst for the project. The prize money would be funded primarily by breeders, who would merely have to breed one additional mare per year to each stallion in order to pay an annual nomination fee. There would be additional, smaller fees paid to make the offspring of each stallion eligible.

The payoff, Gaines believed, would be twofold. Racing would get national exposure of the best kind, a series of races with the top horses in the world. And breeders would profit because the horses they produced would command more in the marketplace, as owners sought runners good enough to compete in these million-dollar events.

By the end of the afternoon, Galbreath was on board. "I'll support you with my stallions," he told Gaines.

Gaines then got positive feedback from the likes of Leslie Combs II of Spendthrift Farm, Charles Taylor of Windfields Farm, owner Nelson Bunker Hunt, Hall of Fame trainer John Nerud, Will Farish of Lane's End Farm, Brereton C. Jones of Airdrie Stud, John T.L. Jones, Jr. of Walmac International, Seth Hancock of Claiborne Farm, and James A. Philpott, Jr., the vice-president and general counsel at Gainesway. By the spring of 1982, he was ready to go public with his idea. On April 23, 1982, Gaines was to be honored at the Kentucky Derby Festival's "They're Off" luncheon in Louisville. That was the place, he decided, to let everyone in on his secret, and announce his grand plan.

The night before the luncheon, Gaines phoned Joe Hirsch, the esteemed columnist for *Daily Racing Form*, and told him to be sure to attend. "This is the most important story you're ever going to write," he told Hirsch.

That day Gaines announced his concept. He called it the Breeders' Cup.

The Breeders' Cup Trophy is a bronze reproduction of the Torrie horse originally created by Giovanni da Bologna in Florence, Italy, in the 16th century. The horse is an ecorche, showing the muscles of the animal in detail. Bologna's original is in the Museum of Fine Arts at the University of Edinburgh in Scotland. The Breeders' Cup Trophy was cast from the original and was directly supervised and approved by the University of Edinburgh for the exclusive use of Breeders' Cup Ltd. The largest version of the trophy is permanently owned by the Breeders' Cup, and is displayed each year at the host track. Replicas of the trophy are given to the owner, breeder, trainer, and jockey of each winning horse.

At the time John Gaines thought of the Breeders' Cup, champions largely were decided in the fall championship races at New York's Belmont Park. Any horse who had raced in the West or Midwest early in the year was often considered unworthy of a championship unless he proved himself in New York. There were only three races worth $1 million in the United States. Cable television was in its infancy. ESPN was a start-up company. FOX Network did not exist. The average fan's exposure to racing on national television was largely confined to the Triple Crown races, and a handful of races shoehorned into anthology shows like ABC's "Wide World of Sports." A void was waiting to be filled.

Just 2 1/2 years after that announcement, the first Breeders' Cup was run, at Hollywood Park on November 10, 1984. The Breeders' Cup has since achieved all that Gaines had envisioned. It is a nationally televised spectacle, encompassing 4 1/2 hours of live television on Saturday afternoon on NBC. Its eight races are a critical factor in determining year-end Eclipse Award championships, both for horses and humans. Breeders' Cup has helped enhance corporate sponsorship in racing, which began with the Marlboro Cup in the 1970s, and now extends to such august events as the Triple Crown.

The Breeders' Cup has allowed fans throughout North America to see racing's greatest stars. The championship event has been held at tracks across the United States, and even in Canada. Some of Europe's premier runners have extended their racing season to run in the Breeders' Cup; without it, horses such as two-time Breeders' Cup winner Miesque likely never would have raced in this country. The races are shown around the world, and simulcast betting on the event extends internationally, too. The Breeders' Cup is racing's World Series, its Super Bowl. Indeed, it is now impossible to consider the sport without such a defining, year-end event.

From the beginning, the Breeders' Cup has been a hit with fans, who come from all over the world to see the greatest racing this sport has to offer.

John Nerud (below) was one of the key players in the founding of the Breeders' Cup. He also was an early winner of a Breeders' Cup race, when his turf star Cozzene (above) won the Breeders' Cup Mile in 1985 at Aqueduct. Cozzene, shown enjoying his retirement (right), went on to be a successful sire, his offspring including Breeders' Cup winners Alphabet Soup and Tikkanen. Years of breeding tradition help produce a Breeders' Cup champion like Capote (opposite page, top). The Hancock family's Claiborne Farm, which has been in racing for generations, has reminders of its great past all over the farm, particularly in the stallion barn, where those who have resided in the first stall, like Secretariat, are remembered. Newer farms, such as Allen Paulson's Brookside Farms (opposite page, bottom), are creating their own legacy by standing at stud horses who achieved success on the racetrack while wearing the Paulson silks.

COZZENE — 1985 Mile

Yet in 1982, reaction to the Breeders' Cup concept was mixed. And there were several moments over the next year when the Breeders' Cup nearly imploded because of such concrete, core issues as funding and support from breeders, to inevitable feuds between racing leaders whose personalities did not mesh.

Many prominent breeders supported Gaines, as did fans and the racing trade press. But smaller breeders were skeptical, as were some nationally prominent press members, and several racetrack executives. But having worked through the potential pitfalls with those he took into his counsel, Gaines was ready for the daunting challenge of getting the Breeders' Cup up and running.

"I had kept it as a closely held idea, based on my experience in a fragmented industry. I realized that to achieve something like this politically, it had to be done quickly and thoroughly," Gaines said, nearly 20 years after he made that historic announcement. "I knew I had to have the people who stood the major stallions involved in this process."

Gaines moved quickly. The board of directors of Breeders' Cup Limited was named on May 3. It included Combs, Gaines, Taylor, and Hancock. Three weeks later, the first officers were named. Gaines was the president, Hancock and Brownell Combs, Leslie's son, were the vice-presidents, Taylor was the secretary, Philpott the assistant secretary, and Brereton C. Jones of Airdrie Stud was the treasurer.

Gaines formed several committees to oversee various aspects of the Breeders' Cup. Top breeders and owners such as Bert Firestone and John Mabee, as well as stallion managers from leading farms, were included. D.G.

Van Clief, Jr. was brought in later that year as the new executive director, replacing Jack Hardy.

"I had a very concrete plan and a mission statement of what I wanted to accomplish for the sport and the industry," Gaines said. "I knew there would be opposition from the Eastern racing establishment. They didn't want anything to happen they couldn't control. And I knew there would be jealousy from the Kentucky hardboots. Those were two political issues to overcome. Both reared their ugly head, but we had solutions, and we had a strong and cohesive group that hung together."

The New York Racing Association, realizing that the importance of its fall championship series might be lessened because of the Breeders' Cup, proposed making its fall championship races the Breeders' Cup races. NYRA wanted to make the Champagne Stakes, for instance, the Breeders' Cup Juvenile Champagne, and make the Jockey Club Gold Cup the Breeders' Cup Classic Jockey Club Gold Cup.

There were other clouds on the horizon. Small breeders in Kentucky were fearful that the Breeders' Cup would simply reward the biggest breeding farms, which had the best stallions and, in theory, were breeding the best horses. Many wanted the Breeders' Cup's funds to go to existing races. A compromise was reached. Half of the money gleaned each year from stallion and foal nominations goes to the annual Championship day. The other half goes to support a series of Breeders' Cup-sponsored stakes races throughout the calendar year at different racetracks.

The division of the funds caused great strife among the early leaders of the Breeders' Cup. Brereton Jones was among those who wanted the money dispersed over the year, believing it would make the Breeders' Cup a better sell to rank-and-file breeders. Bunker Hunt, who, along with Gaines, initially wanted the money to go solely to Championship day purses, was opposed to spreading the money around the country. Hancock did not immediately nominate his stallions, believing the framework of the organization was not solid. Philpott, Arnold Kirkpatrick of Spendthrift Farm, and James E. Friess of Claiborne Farm worked to ease concern over such items as the nomination fee for foals.

Gaines saw that his position with the Breeders' Cup, and with Gainesway, was a lightning rod for controversy. A weekly trade magazine published an article saying, in effect, the Breeders' Cup was dead because of the infighting. On October 22, Gaines resigned as president to become board chairman. C. Gibson Downing, considered a master conciliator who did not favor either side, took over as president. As Nerud said, "He had a tongue as silvery and slick as anyone in the world."

There were other issues that had to be worked through. There was a faction that wanted the Breeders' Cup spread over several days, rather than on one afternoon. Nerud wanted a one-mile race. He got it. But it was placed on the turf, which he did not want, in order to appeal to Europeans. "We couldn't gear the races toward Europe, because Americans put up most of the money," Nerud argued.

Most importantly, Hancock was not on board. He told syndicate members of Claiborne stallions that the horses would not be nominated until questions over how the Breeders' Cup would be operated were answered. Several smaller farms also stood on the sidelines, taking a cue from Claiborne.

A rules committee—including Van Clief, Friess, and Keith Nally of Spendthrift Farm—drafted a 33-page rule book, specifying where the money went and how it was to be spent. Hancock, duly satisfied, urged syndicate members to approve the nomination of Claiborne's stallions. Smaller farms followed Hancock's lead.

"If Claiborne didn't come on board, I don't know if this would have gone ahead, frankly," said Van Clief, who is now the president of Breeders' Cup Ltd. "Claiborne has a very strong leadership role."

Finances were a critical issue in the nascent days of the Breeders' Cup. "We were hanging on by our fingernails," Van Clief recalled.

Nerud said that at one early meeting attended by ten of the founders, Gaines asked for them to each put up $50,000 as operational money. Of course, if the Breeders' Cup failed to go through, the money would be gone. "Six signed on, and four went to the bathroom," Nerud said.

Gaines and Nerud, whose forceful personalities are credited by several insiders with keeping the project moving, went around the country, selling the Breeders' Cup to stallion owners and wary racetrack operators. Money started to come in. By April 15, 1983, 1,083 stallions had been nominated to the program, raising revenue of nearly $11 million. In 1983, only three of the 320 yearlings at the prestigious Keeneland July Sale were not nominated to the Breeders' Cup.

"It didn't cost anybody anything," Gaines said of the breeders. "All they had to do was add one more season to a stallion's book, and send the money to us for the good of the club. It seemed like a painless way to raise significant money.

"The amazing thing," Gaines added, "is that one year from the announcement, we were funded and ready to roll."

The Breeders' Cup also set about finding a host track for the inaugural Championship day. Presentations were made by tracks such as Arlington Park, Atlantic City, Belmont Park, the Meadowlands, and Woodbine, but by the fall of 1982, it had been decided that the event would be held in Southern California, either at Hollywood Park, or Santa Anita's Oak Tree meeting.

Marje Everett, the vice-chairman of the board at Hollywood Park, wanted the event badly. Everett was well-connected, both politically and in the entertainment field. Her presentation dazzled the site selection committee, and on February 24, 1983, Hollywood Park was chosen to play host to the first Breeders' Cup.

Gaines saw network television as a critical component of the Breeders' Cup. At the suggestion of Nerud, two veteran television packagers, Mike Letis and Mike Trager, were brought in to represent the Breeders' Cup and hammer out a deal with the networks. The three major networks—ABC, CBS, and NBC—all made pitches, but it was NBC that immediately embraced the idea of devoting four continuous hours to a one-day Breeders' Cup. On September 13, 1983, the Breeders' Cup and NBC announced the signing of a multi-year deal to broadcast all seven Breeders' Cup races. "This will carry the impact of the Super Bowl and World Series for those involved in the sport of Thoroughbred racing," said then-NBC president Arthur Watson.

The goal of every breeder is to have their youngster grow up to become a champion. For some, the dream begins when a mating is planned, after careful examination of pedigrees and nicks. But a breeder's heart really starts pumping when a young foal takes his first, promising steps, racing through a field on a gorgeous spring day. Might he be a future Breeders' Cup winner? Go ahead, dream a little dream.

In January 1984, the graded stakes panel of the Thoroughbred Owners and Breeders Association made the unprecedented decision to award Grade I status to the Breeders' Cup races. Previously, a race had to be run several times before it could be graded. By now, everyone realized that Breeders' Cup was going to be more than just another day at the races.

Corporate sponsors, such as Mobil Oil, Chrysler, and Anheuser-Busch Inc., signed up that summer. And ten days before the Breeders' Cup, 77 horses were pre-entered in the seven races.

In the days leading up to the event, there was great excitement as horses from all over the world arrived at Hollywood Park to compete. The horses who ran in the inaugural Breeders' Cup had made their most recent starts at Arlington Park, Aqueduct, Bay Meadows, Belmont Park, Del Mar, Keeneland, Laurel, Longacres, Los Alamitos, Louisiana Downs, the Meadowlands, Santa Anita, and Woodbine, and in England, France, and Ireland. The 1983 Horse of the Year, All Along, was there. So, too, Slew o' Gold, who had swept the three-race fall championship series at Belmont Park to become the pro-tem leader for 1984 Horse of the Year.

The week of the inaugural event, Gaines sent out a letter to breeders and owners throughout the nation. "On Championship day, nearly 10,000 owners and breeders will be standing in the winner's circle together with our

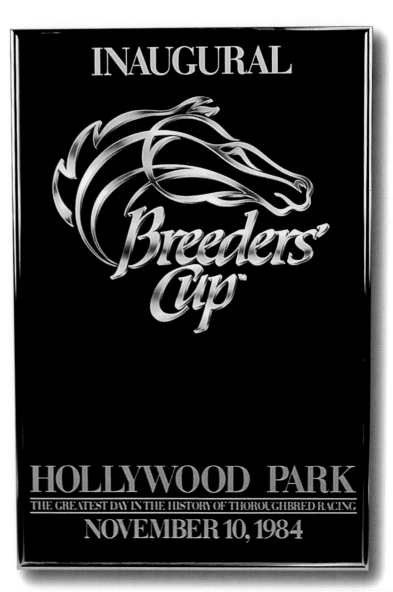

Promotional poster, 1984.

Daily Racing Form, November 10, 1984.

hands joined, one with the other, and our heads raised high," the letter read. "For the first time in the history of our sport, the owners and breeders will have taken charge of their own destiny and accepted responsibility for both the improvement of the breed and the improvement of our sport."

A crowd of 64,254 showed up on a gorgeous, 70-degree fall day at Hollywood Park. Shortly before 11 a.m, the ten runners in the Breeders' Cup Juvenile made their way from the stable area to the paddock. At 11:05, they came onto the racetrack for the post parade. At 11:15, they were put in the starting gate for the one-turn mile race, and then sent on their way.

A racing spectacle unlike any ever seen was about to unfold.

John Henry's saddlecloth.

While the Hollywood celebrities showed up, there was one star who could not make the races on that inaugural Breeders' Cup day. Two-time Horse of the Year John Henry got so close to running that his saddlecloth (above) was produced before he had to miss the big day with an injury, keeping him in the barn (below). But the absence of this popular runner did not diminish the quality of the day's racing, showing from the start that the event is bigger than any one participant.

Celebrities always have been drawn to major sporting events. The inaugural Breeders' Cup proved to be no exception. Those who accepted an invitation to the black-tie party the night before the Breeders' Cup were treated to a brief concert from the legendary Frank Sinatra, one of many stars who attended the Breeders' Cup. Also at Hollywood Park on race day were Burt Bacharach, Joan Collins, Linda Evans, John Forsythe, Cary Grant, Jack Klugman, Gregory Peck, and Elizabeth Taylor (above). They all were invited by Hollywood Park executive Marje Everett, who wanted to add a glamorous touch to the day's racing.

1984 Breeders' Cup winner's medallion.

It was a bright, sunshiny day at Hollywood Park for the inaugural Breeders' Cup. The Breeders' Cup Trophy, an ecorche horse, stood majestically in the paddock (right). The magnitude of the event resulted in a flood of ticket requests, and though tickets were printed, they were never released because of a distribution problem. Just a handful of these rare, uncirculated souvenirs can be found today.

1984 Breeders' Cup admission tickets.

The very first Breeders' Cup race proved as good as advertised. After Chief's Crown (below, center) won the race with jockey Don MacBeth, the colt's trainer, Roger Laurin, presciently said, "The money was not the biggest thing today. This guarantees Chief's Crown the divisional championship." What a field it was! Tank's Prospect (below, right), who finished second, captured the Preakness Stakes the following year. And the colt (below, left) who finished third? Six months later, he won the Kentucky Derby, proving it's great to make a buck, but it's more fun to Spend a Buck. Chief's Crown, owned by the Rosen family's Star Crown Stable, had a great campaign at age 3, too. He finished in the money in all three Triple Crown races, then won the Travers Stakes at Saratoga.

The inaugural Juvenile was an omen. From that race forward, the Breeders' Cup has been the ultimate barometer of class in a racehorse.

1984 Breeders' Cup pre-entry form, Official Track Program, and event pin.

Wild Again was not an original nominee to the Breeders' Cup, so in order for his owners to run him in the inaugural Breeders' Cup Classic at Hollywood Park, they had to put up a supplemental fee of $360,000 when turning in their entry form. The gamble paid off for William Allen, Terry Beal, and Ron Volkman, who raced as the Black Chip Stable, named in honor of the $100 chip at Las Vegas casinos. Before the sun set on a thrilling day of racing, their nearly jet-black colt, a 31-1 longshot, held off Gate Dancer and Slew o' Gold in a thriller. "When Slew o' Gold ranged outside him, I thought he was going to throw in the towel," said jockey Pat Day, who rode Wild Again. "But he pinned his ears and dug in, like he knew Mr. Beal, Mr. Allen, and Mr. Volkman had confidence in him, and he didn't want to let them down. No horse has ever run the final quarter-mile with the determination he did." The wild stretch run, featuring heavy bumping between Wild Again, Slew o' Gold, and Gate Dancer, kept sports fans debating the result long after the official sign was posted.

WILD AGAIN - 1984 Classic

The first Breeders' Cup turned out to be a roaring success. It received sensational coverage nationwide, both in the general press and in trade publications. NBC's unprecedented, four-hour telecast got terrific ratings for a horse-racing show, and was rewarded with the Eclipse Award for national television achievement. John Gaines, founder of the Breeders' Cup, received the Eclipse Award of Merit.

Most importantly, the races had been compelling and unquestionably significant. Chief's Crown, who won the Breeders' Cup Juvenile, was named the champion 2-year-old colt. Outstandingly, who won the Breeders' Cup Juvenile Fillies via disqualification, was the Eclipse Award-winning 2-year-old filly. Princess Rooney, the Breeders' Cup Distaff winner, was the champion older filly or mare. Eillo parlayed his victory in the Breeders' Cup Sprint into an Eclipse Award as champion sprinter. Royal Heroine, who beat the boys in the Breeders' Cup Mile, was named the champion female turf horse. Slew o' Gold, so courageous despite racing on sore hooves in the Breeders' Cup Classic, won the Eclipse Award as champion older horse. And Pat Day, his national profile boosted by his victory aboard Wild Again in the Classic, was named the champion jockey. The Breeders' Cup had accomplished its goal, settling championships on the racetrack.

The success of Europeans such as Lashkari in the Breeders' Cup Turf provided encouragement for subsequent foreigners to extend their season, ship across the Atlantic, and shoot for the million-dollar purses. After just one year, the Breeders' Cup was recognized as the ultimate, year-end prize.

NBC, whose team includes Trevor Denman (above), has broadcast the Breeders' Cup every year, and has been rewarded with both Eclipse Awards and a Sports Emmy (right) for the network's compelling coverage of the 1992 Championship day at Gulfstream Park. Robert Sangster (left), standing next to jockey Fernando Toro after Sangster's Royal Heroine captured the inaugural Breeders' Cup Mile in 1984, was one of the first owners based in Europe to recognize the importance of this event. "It's a little bit late in the season for our top horses, that's the only snag," Sangster said then. "But when the prize money's here, you've got to come."

1992 Sports Emmy Award.

Others who have shared their emotions while enjoying the riches of the Breeders' Cup include trainer Craig Dollase and jockey Corey Nakatani (above); trainer Jenine Sahadi (left); owner Cot Campbell, trainer Nick Zito, and owner Prince Ahmed Salman embracing trainer Alex Hassinger, Jr. (below, left to right); and jockey Jorge Chavez (bottom), showing Artax his appreciation after a victory in the 1999 Breeders' Cup Sprint.

That, in turn, has led to changes in the racing calendar. As trainers became more focused on the Breeders' Cup, which is run annually in late October or early November, they began to campaign their horses differently.

"I find myself giving my horses a late-summer break if they've already had a significant campaign early in the year," said Bill Mott, the Hall of Fame trainer best known for guiding Cigar to a 16-race win streak, including the 1995 Breeders' Cup Classic. "I'll skip a couple of races just to make sure they're fresh enough. But you've also got to really know you've got the right one, otherwise you're better off getting it while you can earlier in the year."

"Getting to Breeders' Cup day is hard. You don't want to stub your toe along the way," said trainer Shug McGaughey, whose Breeders' Cup winners include Personal Ensign, the undefeated winner of the 1988 Breeders' Cup Distaff. "You try not to overdo it. If you think you've got a decent horse, you've got to space the races accordingly, and keep your horse fresh." Trainer Neil Drysdale, whose biggest Breeders' Cup victory came with Horse of the Year A.P. Indy in the 1992 Breeders' Cup Classic, said the Breeders' Cup "has helped the management of horses."

"Trainers realize that they have to have something at the end of the year," Drysdale said. "People are more conservative than they used to be."

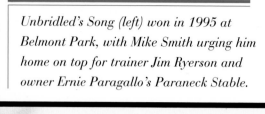

Unbridled's Song (left) won in 1995 at Belmont Park, with Mike Smith urging him home on top for trainer Jim Ryerson and owner Ernie Paragallo's Paraneck Stable.

Horseshoe worn by Unbridled in the 1990 Classic, shown actual size.

1990 Breeders' Cup event pin.

Anees, trained by Alex Hassinger, Jr., rallied from last place to first under jockey Gary Stevens, who was wearing the colors of Prince Ahmed Salman's The Thoroughbred Corporation.

UNBRIDLED - 1990 Classic

One of the great treats of the Breeders' Cup is seeing the offspring of Breeders' Cup race winners follow in the footsteps of their parents. The blaze-faced Unbridled, who was ridden by Pat Day, added a 1990 Breeders' Cup Classic win to his victory in that year's Kentucky Derby for trainer Carl Nafzger and owner Frances Genter. Nafzger, who gave Unbridled a brief vacation following that year's Triple Crown, was one of the first trainers to recognize the importance of the Breeders' Cup and point specifically for it. Unbridled's legacy has lived on through the years. His sons Unbridled's Song and Anees made papa proud by winning the Breeders' Cup Juvenile.

Racetracks also had to alter their schedules to accommodate the Breeders' Cup. Belmont Park's fall championship series, and Santa Anita's Oak Tree meeting—both of which race in October—reconfigured their stakes programs in order to make their biggest races timely preps for the Breeders' Cup. And tracks that raced soon after the Breeders' Cup, such as Santa Anita's winter meeting, also felt the effects.

"Most definitely it changed Oak Tree and Santa Anita both," said Tom Robbins, the former vice-president of racing at Santa Anita. "We used to put the major focus of the Oak Tree meeting in late October or early November prior to 1984, but we had to move those stakes forward, to the beginning of the meet, so they could be used as stepping stones to the Breeders' Cup. All tracks running at that time have to do the same thing. And you're in competition, because if you ignore those horses, they'll just go to other parts of the country.

"It's a little more subtle at Santa Anita," Robbins added. "Some horses aren't geared up early in the meet, because if they run in the Breeders' Cup, they start later. Trainers recognize that you can't go hard 12 months a year.

Racetracks compete for the right to play host to Breeders' Cup Championship day; knowing the event brings prestige to the racecourse, and millions of dollars in revenue to the surrounding community. Woodbine (above left) and Santa Anita (below left) have been Breeders' Cup sites, along with Hollywood Park (above), which had the inaugural Breeders' Cup in 1984.

Nothing has captured the desires of horsemen in this country like the Breeders' Cup. Everybody wants to be a part of it. Tracks have been impacted by it, but it's a good sacrifice."

Belmont Park decided to join, rather than fight, the Breeders' Cup. Allen Gutterman, the New York Racing

Association's former marketing chief, created Super Saturday, in which the fall meet's premier races were run on one day, about one month before the Breeders' Cup. It served as both an ideal prep, and a glorious day of racing on its own.

Race distances have been altered. Belmont Park's Jockey Club Gold Cup was once a two-mile race. It was still 1 1/2 miles in 1989. After Easy Goer lost that year's Breeders' Cup Classic to Sunday Silence, the Jockey Club Gold Cup was shortened again, to 1 1/4 miles. The Washington D.C. International, once the elite turf race in the U.S., is no more.

The preparation for a Breeders' Cup win begins early in the week, in the quiet of the morning, when the horses and their handlers bond in a tranquil setting, training for the battle that will be at hand on Saturday afternoon.

"The Breeders' Cup has been a great help in defining championships. And what price do you put on four hours of live television?" said Lenny Hale, who was a senior vice-president for the New York Racing Association when Aqueduct played host to the second Breeders' Cup in 1985. "It's been helpful and harmful, but overall I think it's one of the best things that has happened in racing in a long time."

The Breeders' Cup also has made adjustments. The Breeders' Cup Distaff was shortened from 1 1/4 miles to 1 1/8 miles to make it more aligned with races for that division the rest of the year. The purse of the Breeders' Cup Classic was raised to $4 million. The Breeders' Cup Distaff's purse doubled, to $2 million. A new race, the $1 million Breeders' Cup Filly and Mare Turf, began in 1999. Total prize money on Championship day is now $13 million. The Breeders' Cup Steeplechase, which never was part of the on-site program with the races on the flat, was discontinued after 1993, then reintroduced in 2000.

Rules regarding supplementary nominations were tweaked, and for the better. At the outset of the Breeders' Cup, owners of horses not nominated to the Breeders' Cup had to pay stiff supplementary fees to race each year. It is still far more cost-effective to pay the smaller fees early in the nominating process, but the supplementary rules are less pernicious. Now, the supplementary fee only has to be paid once, not every year. In addition, the supplementary money is added to the race purse.

"I worked a long time to overcome that," said trainer Ron McAnally, whose mare Bayakoa had to be supplemented twice to the Breeders' Cup Distaff by owners Frank and Jan Whitham.

Chris McCarron

Bill Shoemaker

Mike Smith

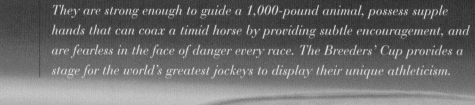
They are strong enough to guide a 1,000-pound animal, possess supple hands that can coax a timid horse by providing subtle encouragement, and are fearless in the face of danger every race. The Breeders' Cup provides a stage for the world's greatest jockeys to display their unique athleticism.

Jose Santos

Craig Perret

Jorge Chavez

Laffit Pincay, Jr.

Pat Eddery

Lester Piggott

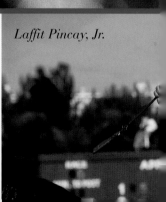

Gary Stevens

Eddie Delahoussaye

Pat Valenzuela

Corey Nakatani

Pat Day

Jerry Bailey

Randy Romero

Angel Cordero, Jr.

James E. (Ted) Bassett III (above) took over as the president of Breeders' Cup Limited in 1988, succeeding C. Gibson Downing, and guided the Breeders' Cup through an explosive growth period. On-track handle on the inaugural Breeders' Cup races in 1984 was $8,443,070. The overall total, including simulcast outlets, was $16,452,479. In 1988, the proliferation of simulcasting resulted in $42,932,379 being bet on the races. In 1996, that total swelled to $67,738,890. In December 1996, when Bassett retired, and D.G. Van Clief, Jr., was voted president, the Breeders' Cup was firmly established as racing's championship day. In 1999, the Breeders' Cup had its first $100-million day.

The Breeders' Cup has influence throughout the year, too. The National Stakes program has continued to prosper. The year 2000 program encompassed 54 graded stakes worth more than $46.5 million.

Championship day has been and will be the focal point of the Breeders' Cup program. Races such as the 1987 Breeders' Cup Classic (right) in which Ferdinand, number 6, held off Alysheba, number 9, in a rare battle of two Kentucky Derby winners, have settled championships where they should be settled, on the track. Horses such as 1996 Breeders' Cup Sprint winner Lit de Justice (below) might never have had their talent fully appreciated had the Breeders' Cup not provided the stage.

A tip of the hat to the Breeders' Cup. Because it attracts a mix of cultures from around the world, the Breeders' Cup has developed its own cosmopolitan sense of haute couture. As with the Kentucky Derby, women accessorize stylishly, with elegant hats and designer sunglasses.

The Breeders' Cup has continued to grow in popularity, both in terms of media coverage and fan participation. NBC, which has been there from the start, has expanded its live telecast to 4 1/2 hours. NBC also has a show on Breeders' Cup Preview Day from Belmont Park, and ESPN has its popular "Racing to the Breeders' Cup" series of telecasts. Hundreds of journalists converge on the Breeders' Cup every year from Asia, Europe, Australia, and North America. Advances in simulcasting allow fans throughout the continent, and even internationally, to wager on the races. Fans can bet on a pick six that in 1999 had a guaranteed pool of $5 million, a bigger prize than the horses chase in the Breeders' Cup Classic.

The Breeders' Cup is a star-studded affair. It attracts world-renowned artists, athletes, and actors. Among those who have joined the crowd for a great day of Breeders' Cup racing (above, clockwise from center) are former President Gerald Ford and his wife, Betty, hosted by noted owner and breeder Allen Paulson; author Dick Francis, actor Mel Brooks, Playboy founder Hugh Hefner and a few of his close friends, quarterback turned television analyst Terry Bradshaw, and the popular sporting artist, Leroy Neiman (top) with one of his paintings.

1997 press party invitation.

The attraction, from the very beginning, has been the horses. Get the very best from the world over, prepared by the best trainers, ridden by the best jockeys, and you have an annual day of racing that is second to none.

(Left to right) The 1998 Breeders' Cup Classic field and their lifetime earnings (*as of June 15, 2000). Victory Gallop (not shown) earned $3,505,895.

The greatest field assembled for a Breeders' Cup race was the 1998 Breeders' Cup Classic at Churchill Downs. The field included the winners of the Kentucky Derby, Preakness Stakes, Belmont Stakes, Dubai World Cup, Blue Grass Stakes, Donn Handicap, Gulfstream Park Handicap, Haskell Invitational, Hollywood Gold Cup, Jockey Club Gold Cup, Pacific Classic, Pimlico Special, Super Derby, Travers Stakes, Whitney Handicap, Woodbine Million, Woodward Stakes, several Group I races in Europe, and the previous year's Breeders' Cup Classic. Of the 10 runners, five had been or would be voted year-end championships. They earned a total of nearly $40 million during their careers. Befitting such a field, the purse was a Breeders' Cup record $5.12 million. And it lived up to its expectations, with a breathtaking stretch run that found the first five finishers separated by less than two lengths at the wire. In a slight upset, Awesome Again, who had won all five of his previous starts that year, rallied boldly and split horses under jockey Pat Day to beat Silver Charm by three-quarters of a length, with European star Swain a close third. Awesome Again, expertly managed all year by trainer Patrick Byrne, was led into the winner's circle (below) by Frank Stronach, who bred and owned the colt.

Coronado's Quest $2,046,190

Swain (Ire) $3,777,115

…h $480,990

Awesome Again $4,374,590

III. Players

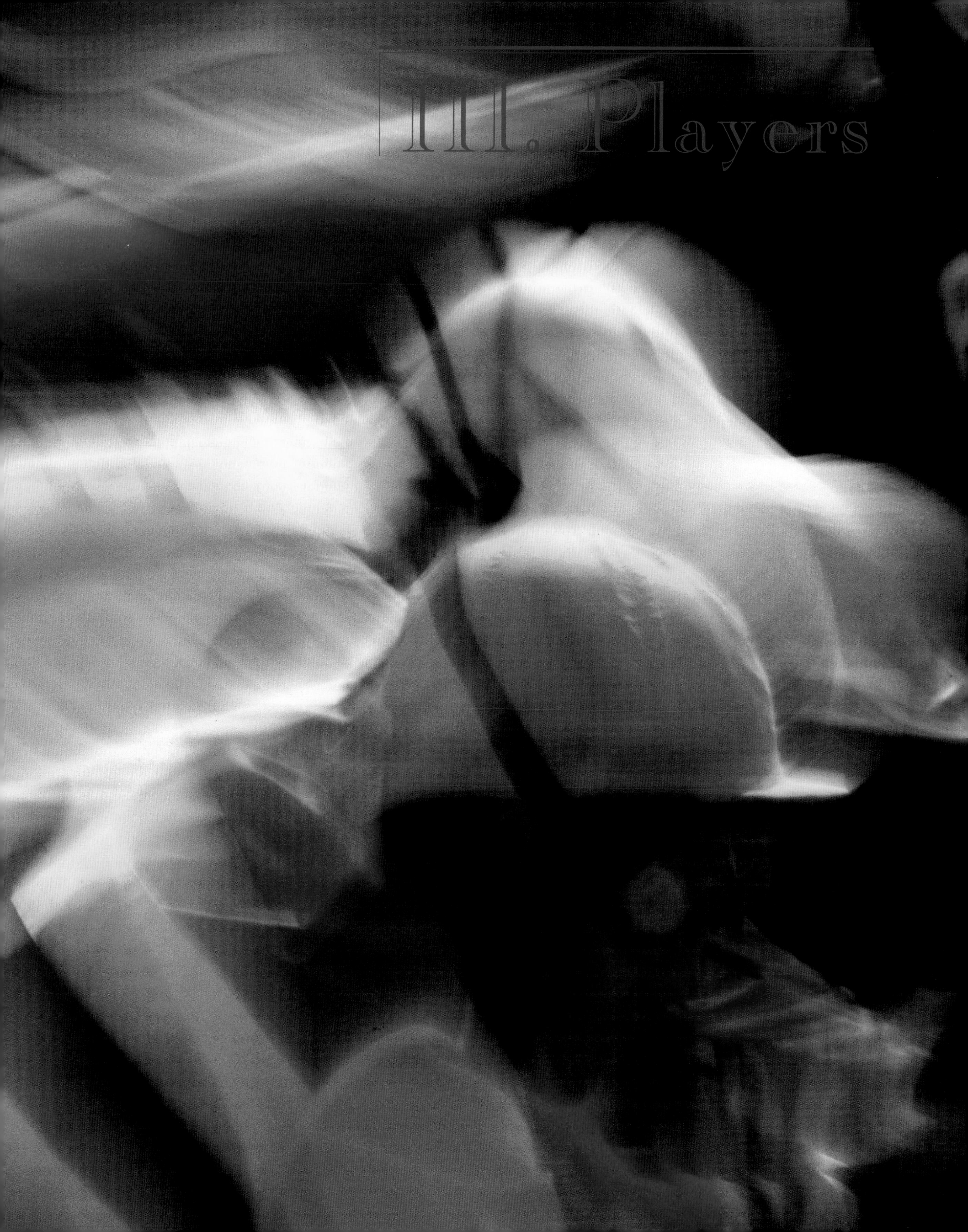

The Breeders' Cup was designed to determine national championships, the most coveted of which is Horse of the Year. Owners of the Horse of the Year receive a gold Eclipse Award statue, signifying that their horse was the best in the land. In its first 16 runnings, the Breeders' Cup featured that year's Horse of the Year 11 times. The winners included both an older star and a precocious colt who had perfect seasons, and a dainty filly whose iron constitution carried her to victories from one end of the country to the other. We raise a glass and offer them a toast.

SMOKE ON THE WATER

Bill Mott has a placid exterior, but inside, he was churning. The trainer had guided Cigar to a perfect year, 9-for-9. Combined with two victories at the end of the previous year, Cigar had won 11 straight races. But as the 1995 Breeders' Cup Classic approached, Mott was nervous. Cigar never had raced on an off track, and weather forecasters had been predicting rain all week for Championship day at Belmont Park. Their handicapping was right on target.

"It was an unknown factor," Mott recalled. "I didn't know how he'd handle it. The night before the race, our barn was completely flooded out. We were scooping water out. We dug ourselves out of the swamp and took him to the training track."

All of a sudden, Mott's worries melted away.

"He went so good," Mott said. "His tail was up over his back. I thought, 'This son of a gun is going to handle it.' I just quit worrying. At that point, a switch went on. It gave me some confidence. He had already won 11 in a row, and I really wanted him to have a perfect year. The tension built inside me for each race, and now here was the big one."

The Belmont main track was muddy, but there was solid footing under the layer of mud, and the track was producing fast times. Cigar, favored at 7-10 by the crowd of 37,246, was close to the pace while wide during the early going. Jerry Bailey, his rider, had a snug hold, and

Cigar was tugging hard at the bit. "Cigar wants to go to the lead, but Jerry Bailey says no, not yet," track announcer Tom Durkin said.

"And then he turned him loose, and he looked like he was shot out of a slingshot," Mott said.

If you have a Cigar, you're going to go far. Maybe not to the dark side of the moon, but halfway around the world, and all over the country. His talented team included jockey Jerry Bailey (left), owner Allen Paulson, and trainer Bill Mott (right). Below: Cigar training at Belmont Park.

Smokin'! Steam rises from the glistening coat of Cigar while he gets a nice, warm bath following his morning exercise. Cigar's success helped propel both his jockey, Jerry Bailey, and his trainer, Bill Mott, into the National Museum of Racing and Hall of Fame. He won 19 of 33 starts and retired with lifetime earnings of $9,999,815, a record.

Cigar was sheer perfection in 1995, when he won all 10 of his starts. He skipped effortlessly over the muddy Belmont Park track en route to this victory (below and right) in the Breeders' Cup Classic, which clinched the first of his two titles as Horse of the Year.

In an instant, Cigar—racing in the red, white, and blue silks of his owner and breeder, airplane entrepreneur Allen Paulson—moved powerfully while four paths wide to go for the lead. He went from fourth to first while rounding the final turn. A piece of machinery used to groom the track between races had left grooved tire tracks on the dirt, and Bailey cleverly kept Cigar along that path, all the way to the finish line. It was Bailey's third straight victory in the Classic.

Cigar was named Horse of the Year. The next year, Cigar ran his winning streak to 16, including a stirring victory in the inaugural Dubai World Cup, run halfway around the world in the United Arab Emirates. And though he lost his final career start in the 1996 Breeders' Cup Classic, Cigar was a repeat winner as Horse of the Year.

Mott trained Cigar for 24 races, and won 17. He says the 1995 Classic was Cigar's finest hour.

"It was very meaningful," Mott said. "It was probably his biggest win, because it meant a perfect season, 10-for-10, and Horse of the Year. It was probably more important even than Dubai. Dubai was important. Don't get me wrong. But there's something about a perfect season."

"He looked like he was shot out of a slingshot."

BLACK TIE AFFAIR (Ire) - 1991 Classic

Formal attire was needed in 1991, when Jeffrey Sullivan's Black Tie Affair led from start to finish in the Breeders' Cup Classic, a victory that proved decisive in his being voted Horse of the Year. Jockey Jerry Bailey, taking advantage of a paceless race, sent Black Tie Affair to the front, coaxed him through moderate fractions, and saved plenty for the long stretch run at Churchill Downs. For Bailey, it was his first win in the Classic, a race he would win three more times in the next four years. Black Tie Affair, trained by Ernie Poulos, was remarkably versatile. He finished third in the Breeders' Cup Sprint in 1990 at Belmont Park, but found his best form the following year at age 5, when he won 7 of 10 starts.

KOTASHAAN (Fr) - 1993 Turf

The pressure was on Kotashaan and
jockey Kent Desormeaux in the 1993
Breeders' Cup Turf at Santa Anita.
The year had been dominated by
grass runners, and conventional wisdom held that the nation's top turf
runner stood an excellent chance of
being named Horse of the Year. One
hour before Kotashaan's race, Lure
had scored a front-running victory in
the Breeders' Cup Mile, stamping him
as a legitimate contender for Horse of
the Year. Kotashaan had to win, or
Lure would be a lock. Desormeaux
took no chances. Kotashaan (far left)
went wide throughout, losing valuable
ground, but he proved his superiority
by overpowering arch-rival Bien Bien
in the final furlong to win by a half-
length (below). The victory capped one
of the greatest training feats in the
career of Richard Mandella, who won
four races that afternoon at Santa
Anita, including the Breeders' Cup
Juvenile Fillies with Phone Chatter.

TRICK AND TREAT

A perfect season was the goal for Favorite Trick when he arrived at the Breeders' Cup in 1997 at Hollywood Park. The 2-year-old colt began his campaign sprinting 4 1/2 furlongs in April at Keeneland, remained unbeaten through the summer at Saratoga, and had stretched out successfully around two turns, to 1 1/16 miles, at Keeneland in the fall. He was 7 for 7.

His trainer, Pat Byrne, was having a breakout year. In the spring, Byrne won with a stunning 14 of 17 starters at Churchill Downs. He had won five of the six juvenile stakes run at Saratoga. But none of that mattered now to Byrne. He wanted Favorite Trick to be recognized not only as the best 2-year-old in the country, but as the best horse, period.

"What was stressful, my only concern, is that he had beaten everybody, but people were only saying that if he wins, he should just be the champion 2-year-old. To me, in light of the year, he should have been considered for Horse of the Year," Byrne recalled. "I thought they were counting the horse real short."

Since the inception of the Eclipse Awards in 1971, only Secretariat, in 1972, had been voted Horse of the Year at age 2. Byrne knew Favorite Trick needed a knockout performance to overcome the inherent bias of Eclipse Award voters, who are reluctant to support a 2-year-old for Horse of the Year.

Favorite Trick delivered a crushing blow. His primary rival, Grand Slam, suffered a deep, nasty cut on his left rear leg when clipped by the front legs of Johnbill on the first turn. With that colt eliminated, Favorite Trick had no serious competition. He cruised to the lead effortlessly on the final turn, then bounded clear to win by an emphatic 5 1/2 lengths.

Byrne, acting cocky, was caught by NBC's cameras saying, "There's the Horse of the Year, right there," as Favorite Trick flashed under the wire.

"Wasn't that good?" he asked years later. "I really felt that way."

The magician behind the perfect year for Favorite Trick in 1997 was trainer Pat Byrne (above), who kept the 2-year-old colt (below) in top form from April through November. In the Breeders' Cup Juvenile at Hollywood Park (right), jockey Pat Day merely had to point Favorite Trick in the right direction.

So did the voters. In a controversial decision, Favorite Trick beat Skip Away, that year's champion older horse and Breeders' Cup Classic winner, in balloting for Horse of the Year. It should have been a time to celebrate

FAVORITE TRICK - 1997 Juvenile

for Byrne and Joseph LaCombe, Favorite Trick's owner, but relations between the two were starting to fray. At the end of 1997, Byrne took a private training job with Frank Stronach. LaCombe transferred Favorite Trick to the barn of Bill Mott, who trained the colt during his 3-year-old season.

"Favorite Trick was a special horse," Byrne said. "I hope I get another one like that."

Like a child born into money, A.P. Indy was supposed to have it all. He was sired by Seattle Slew, the 1977 Triple Crown winner, and was out of the dam Weekend Surprise—a daughter of another Triple Crown winner, Secretariat—who already had produced a classic winner in Summer Squall, the 1990 Preakness Stakes winner. At the 1990 summer sales, just two months after Summer Squall's Preakness victory, A.P. Indy was sold to Japanese businessman Tomonuri Tsurumaki for $2.9 million, the highest price for a yearling sold at auction that year.

A.P. Indy lived up to expectations, winning the Hollywood Futurity at 2 and the Santa Anita Derby at 3.

But the rest of 1992 was a struggle, as his trainer, Neil Drysdale, battled to overcome A.P. Indy's nagging physical problems.

The trouble began the morning of the Kentucky Derby, when Drysdale had to scratch A.P. Indy because of a bothersome foot. He had made it to Churchill Downs, but had to bow out of America's premier race, a devastating blow. When longshot Lil E. Tee won that afternoon, with favored Arazi far back in eighth, Drysdale could only wonder what might have been.

A.P. Indy had a quarter crack, which required a fiberglass patch to protect. The colt raced with it and won the Belmont Stakes. But that fall, he struggled over a dry, loose track in the Molson Million at Woodbine, then nearly did a somersault coming out of the gate in the Jockey Club Gold Cup at Belmont Park.

"He pulled a shoe off. His foot was shredded," Drysdale said. "It looked like someone had taken thick sandpaper and sanded off his foot. The walls were gone."

Drysdale called in a farrier, Joey Carroll, who rebuilt the foot, using an acrylic resin that dries quickly and is hard and resilient. A.P. Indy was then sent to Florida to prepare for the Breeders' Cup Classic at Gulfstream Park. From that point on, everything went smoothly. It was as if A.P. Indy was finally being rewarded for his perseverance, and Drysdale his patience.

"Everything came together for the Breeders' Cup," Drysdale said. "He trained into the race very well. He was spot on."

A.P. Indy was a handful before the Classic, and had to be saddled in the tunnel leading from the paddock to the track. He saved plenty of energy for the race, though. A.P. Indy, his head low to the ground, as if he was searching for a contact lens, knifed between horses on the final turn, then drew away, with his jockey, Eddie Delahoussaye, never having to reach for the whip. It was the exclamation point on a resumé that earned A.P. Indy the Horse of the Year title.

"I thought he dominated the race," Drysdale said. "We had had some difficult moments during the year, but I don't think anyone lost faith in the horse. It's always satisfying when everything turns out."

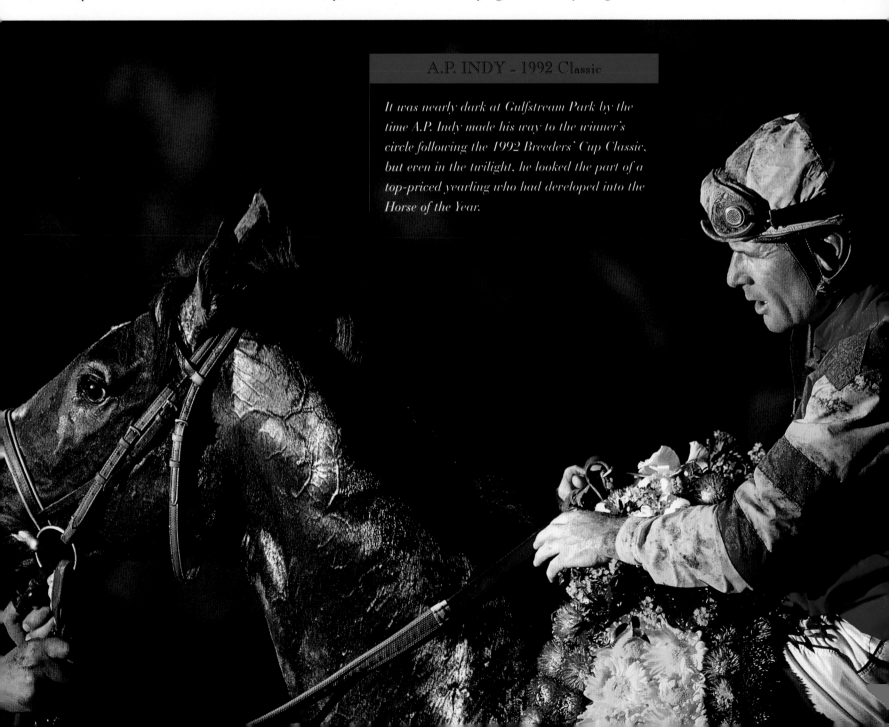

A.P. INDY - 1992 Classic

It was nearly dark at Gulfstream Park by the time A.P. Indy made his way to the winner's circle following the 1992 Breeders' Cup Classic, but even in the twilight, he looked the part of a top-priced yearling who had developed into the Horse of the Year.

Secretariat (right) is considered one of the greatest racehorses of all-time. He was the Triple Crown winner in 1973, and Horse of the Year in both 1972 and 1973. But his influence in the breeding shed has been underappreciated. His name shows up in the pedigrees of many Breeders' Cup winners, including Chief Bearhart, Chief's Crown, Da Hoss, Desert Stormer, Flanders, Storm Song, and A.P. Indy (below), the 1992 Horse of the Year by virtue of his victory in that year's Breeders' Cup Classic at Gulfstream Park.

Although Secretariat was big and robust—experts say he was the perfectly proportioned racing machine—one of his best runners was a dainty, gray-colored filly named Lady's Secret (right). She might not have looked like her sire, but she inherited his will to win, and joined her proud papa as a Horse of the Year by capturing the 1986 Breeders' Cup Distaff at Santa Anita.

Lady's Secret was so small and cuddly, you just wanted to hug her. But all she wanted to do was run. The gray mighty mite ran 45 times and won 25 in a stellar career that spanned four seasons, stamped her as the most accomplished runner sired by Secretariat, and earned her admission into the Hall of Fame.

She finished second to Life's Magic, her D. Wayne Lukas-trained stablemate, in the 1985 Breeders' Cup Distaff at Aqueduct, but the next year, she put on her traveling shoes and went from understudy to top billing.

Lady's Secret won 10 of 15 starts—13 of which were in Grade 1 races—while competing in both New York and California, and challenging males on several occasions. She won a remarkable eight Grade 1 races, including the Whitney Handicap against the boys at Saratoga. Lady's Secret swept Belmont Park's fall series for older fillies and mares—the Maskette, Ruffian and Beldame—for the second straight year, then headed to Santa Anita, where she and stablemate Twilight Ridge were favored at 1-2 in the Distaff.

The race was no contest. Lady's Secret was up by as many as five lengths midway through the 1 1/4-mile race, and just jogged home under a hand ride from her jockey, Pat Day.

"I think we could run her again this afternoon," her proud owner, Gene Klein, said in the winner's circle. "She's just amazing. The Iron Lady. She's got to be the best that ever ran."

She was certainly the best that year. Voters elected Lady's Secret the Horse of the Year.

"Pound for pound, she's the best," Lukas said. "She is a natural athlete blessed with a very rare gift. Lady's Secret is something special."

1986 Breeders' Cup admission ticket and event pin.

LADY'S SECRET – 1986 Distaff

Lady's Secret always made winning look effortless. She would set steady, demanding fractions that her rivals could not match over the length of the race. But a fire burned inside. "She was a real pleasure to ride," said her jockey, Pat Day, who was aboard for this victory in the 1986 Breeders' Cup Distaff. "When she left the gate, she'd pin her ears like a savage. Her body was relaxed, but she'd pin her ears the whole way. She was very competitive."

AT THE WIRE

Sam Janney worked at Hollywood Park for nearly 40 years. His assignment was to hang prints of the photo finish at various locations around the track. Janney was the Yogi Berra of the racetrack, prone to curious twists of phrase. According to long-time Southern California steward Pete Pedersen, Janney, after making the rounds with pictures of a dead heat one day, told the track's stewards, "I've hung a lot of dead heats in my day, but boy, that last one was really close." The Breeders' Cup has had some really close finishes, too. No dead heats, but plenty of races that were picture perfect.

DERBY DUELISTS

Ferdinand won the Kentucky Derby in 1986. Alysheba won it in 1987. Since the value of a colt skyrockets when he wins the Derby, it is rare for two winners to meet, since the older horse often is whisked off to stud. When Ferdinand and Alysheba met for the first time in the 1987 Breeders' Cup Classic at Hollywood Park, it marked only the seventh race between Kentucky Derby winners since 1950, and the first time it had happened in the Breeders' Cup.

This race had significant ramifications, because if either won, he would be Horse of the Year. Ferdinand, after starting the year with six consecutive losses, had won

three straight stakes races—including the Hollywood Gold Cup—for his trainer, Charlie Whittingham, who called his colt "the best horse in America running today."

Alysheba had gone on to win the Preakness Stakes and the Super Derby, and had trained brilliantly for the Classic for trainer Jack Van Berg. "If he beats these horses, I would sure think he'd be Horse of the Year," Van Berg said.

A crowd of 57,734 showed up at Hollywood Park that year on a gorgeous afternoon for this unique showdown. But no one could have anticipated just how great a race they would see.

Ferdinand, the even-money favorite, settled into mid-pack early with his jockey, Bill Shoemaker, while Candi's Gold and Judge Angelucci set the pace in the 1 1/4-mile race. Alysheba, the second choice at 7-2, was farther back under Chris McCarron and was racing wide. Ferdinand crept closer on the final turn, and looked ready to move for the lead at any time. But Shoemaker waited, waited, and waited, finally asking Ferdinand for his best with 100 yards to go.

"He's not an easy horse to ride," Shoemaker said. "When he gets in front, he thinks he's won, and he eases up. You have to time it just right."

Ferdinand took the lead, but as soon as he got past Judge Angelucci, his ears went straight up in the air, signaling he was waiting for competition. He did not have to wait long. By now, Alysheba was flying on the outside, propelled by McCarron's whipping. The two Derby winners surged for the wire and hit it as one, with Ferdinand winning by a nose.

For Shoemaker, it was his only win in the Breeders' Cup. And it made up for a heartbreaking defeat earlier in the day, when he and Whittingham lost the Juvenile Fillies in the final jump, after Jeanne Jones blew a six-length lead at mid-stretch and was nailed by Epitome.

"I'm glad we won this race," said Whittingham, who had lost four races on that year's card prior to the Classic. "I tried all day today, and my pants were getting shorter every race."

The photo finish proved the difference for Horse of the Year, which went to Ferdinand. And as dusk settled on Hollywood Park that afternoon, the Classic's photo was posted throughout the track. Another close one, Sam Janney must have thought.

The finish of the 1987 Breeders' Cup Classic was so close that neither jockey thought he had won. Both Chris McCarron and Bill Shoemaker made a pact to compensate whomever lost, since the winning jockey was to get $135,000, and the second-place finisher $67,500.

"Let's save," McCarron yelled to Shoemaker after the horses crossed the wire. "How about $5,000?"

"Make it $10,000," Shoemaker shot back.

The photo finish showed Ferdinand the winner by the narrowest of margins.

"I owe you $10,000," Shoemaker said to McCarron when he returned to the jockeys' room. McCarron, first in line to congratulate Shoemaker, shook his head and smiled as the 56-year-old Shoemaker walked away.

"He's too much, that little son of a bitch," McCarron said.

FERDINAND - 1987 Classic

Phone Chatter (number 6) literally eclipsed arch-rival Sardula when she got up in the final stride under jockey Laffit Pincay, Jr. to capture the 1993 Breeders' Cup Juvenile Fillies at Santa Anita. The massive daughter of Phone Trick towered over her contemporaries, and cast a long shadow over her division. She was voted the champion 2-year-old filly of 1993, avenging her sire, who never won an Eclipse Award despite being one of the premier sprinters of the mid-1980s. Phone Chatter was owned and bred by Herman Sarkowsky and was trained by Richard Mandella, who later that day sent out Horse of the Year Kotashaan to take the Breeders' Cup Turf.

Fillies such as Very Subtle, Desert Stormer, Soviet Problem, and Meafara have made the six-furlong Sprint the Breeders' Cup dirt race in which fillies have competed most notably against males. But none has been as successful as Safely Kept, who lost narrowly in 1989 at Gulfstream Park, then returned in 1990 at Belmont Park and saw her perseverance pay off.

For Safely Kept, the Sprint results were never in line with the Eclipse Award—Safely Kept was voted the champion sprinter in 1989, then lost in 1990 to Housebuster—but that was about the only thing that was off-kilter during her brilliant career, which saw Safely Kept win 24 of 31 starts.

"She was a great filly, a freak," remembered Craig Perret, who was Safely Kept's regular rider. "Alan Goldberg did a superb job training her. He always placed her in the right races."

After carefully spotting her throughout 1989, Safely Kept was ready for a brilliant effort in that year's Breeders' Cup Sprint. But after setting blazing fractions while dueling with Olympic Prospect, she was caught in the final jump by Dancing Spree.

The next year, Safely Kept again found herself locked in a duel. Only this time, her rival would not go away. She was matched up against Dayjur, who arrived in the United States with a reputation as being the best sprinter in Europe in years. He was that year's champion sprinter in Europe, and his all-American pedigree suggested he would smoothly handle the switch from turf to dirt. They hooked up early in the race, and were virtually inseparable heading into the final sixteenth. "He got about a neck in front of me," Perret recalled. "She was trying, but she had no more to offer."

But then Dayjur decided to audition to be a steeplechaser. Only 40 yards from the finish, he was startled by a shadow that had been cast by the grandstand, and leaped. Safely Kept pounced on him like a cat chasing a bird, and re-rallied to win by a neck.

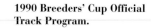

1990 Breeders' Cup Official Track Program.

Dayjur (number 11) and jockey Willie Carson move up to engage Safely Kept (number 5) and Craig Perret at the top of the stretch of the 1990 Breeders' Cup Sprint.

Safely Kept just failed to hold off the late rush of Dancing Spree (left) in the 1989 Breeders' Cup Sprint. The next year (right) at Belmont Park, however, fate smiled on her. Dayjur was moving for the lead when he jumped shadows, allowing Safely Kept to come back along the inside to win by a neck. "If the race had been 20 minutes earlier, or a half-hour later, that shadow wouldn't have been there," said Safely Kept's jockey, Craig Perret. "It was a one-in-a-million chance. It was a gift. Like looking down on the ground and finding a lotto ticket. But she earned it."

Standing in the shadows of love, waiting for the heartache to come. Dayjur, owned by Sheikh Hamdan al Maktoum of Dubai and trained in England by Major Dick Hern, was considered the premier sprinter in Europe in 1990. His adoring fans sent him off as the favorite at 2-1, but his infamous, mid-stretch hop (below) cost him the race. Only moments earlier, Dayjur and jockey Willie Carson left the paddock (above), the lack of sunlight foreshadowing the events that would soon unfold. Safely Kept, owned by Richard Santulli's Jayeff B. Stable, was opportunistic (bottom) as she responded to the left-handed whipping of jockey Craig Perret to get up and win. Their duel (opposite page) remains one of the most memorable races in Breeders' Cup history.

"It was a one-in-a-million chance."

SAFELY KEPT - 1990 Sprint

HOLLYWOOD WILDCAT - 1993 Distaff

The Breeders' Cup returned to spectacular Santa Anita (above) for a second time in 1993. One of the highlights that day was the Breeders' Cup Distaff. Despite losing his whip just before the finish, jockey Eddie Delahoussaye was able to keep Hollywood Wildcat (left) in front to hold off Paseana. Hollywood Wildcat was bred and owned by Irving and Marjorie Cowan, and was trained by Neil Drysdale. This victory clinched for Hollywood Wildcat the Eclipse Award as champion 3-year-old filly. Delahoussaye (below) rode Hollywood Wildcat with a light touch, which allowed her to gain confidence before asking her for her best.

MANILA IN A THRILLA

There was nowhere to run, and Jose Santos wanted to hide. With a furlong remaining in the 1986 Breeders' Cup Turf at Santa Anita, Santos was charging through along the rail with Manila when the hole suddenly closed. Manila already had left Dancing Brave—the European champion, Arc de Triomphe winner, and 1-2 favorite—at the top of the stretch, but two future champions, Theatrical and the mare Estrapade, had the jump on him, and were still running at full speed when Manila ran into a roadblock.

"For a second I thought he would never get up," Santos recalled. "I took a strong hold of him, looked back, pushed him outside, and he found another gear. I hit him, and he took off like he had broken out of the gate again."

Manila had clear sailing during a workout (above) just days before the 1986 Breeders' Cup Turf at Santa Anita, but he had to overcome severe traffic trouble to win the race. After getting stopped at mid-stretch, Manila shifted outside (below) and accelerated strongly to roar past Theatrical (right) and win going away under Jose Santos. LeRoy Jolley trained Manila for owner Mike Shannon.

Time was running out. But Manila, now in the middle of the course, accelerated in an instant, flew past Estrapade, then took aim at Theatrical.

"Gary Stevens was riding Theatrical. He was hitting his horse right-handed, and he accidentally hit my left hand and knocked my stick out of my hand," Santos said. "All that trouble Manila had in the race, and he still won."

No horse in Breeders' Cup history has encountered so much trouble so late in a race and still prevailed. The victory was the eighth in ten starts that year for Manila, who earned the Eclipse Award as champion male turf horse.

"I rode him five times and never got beat with him," Santos said. "He beat all the champions in the Breeders' Cup. When people ask me who's the best turf horse I've ridden, I say Manila."

MANILA - 1986 Turf

ALPHABET SOUP - 1996 Classic

Cigar was trying to win his second straight Breeders' Cup Classic, in 1996 at Woodbine, but the roan-colored horse Alphabet Soup would not let him by. Alphabet Soup, racing between horses in the stretch run, had to hold off Cigar on his outside and Louis Quatorze on his inside to prevail in a photo finish.

The day before the 1996 Breeders' Cup Classic at Woodbine, Alphabet Soup was sent by his trainer, David Hofmans, to the paddock for a schooling session. Often a horse who would fidget and play, Hofmans noticed that Alphabet Soup was quiet that day.

"He got so serious. He stopped playing. Everybody noticed. At home he would walk along and screw off, but he had an intensity about him for two days," Hofmans remembered. "He was so focused."

Alphabet Soup had turned into a professional racehorse, and not a moment too soon. He was facing Cigar, who had won the Classic the previous year, as well as Preakness Stakes winner Louis Quatorze, the crack 3-year-old Will's Way, and Dare And Go, who had stopped Cigar's 16-race winning streak earlier in the Pacific Classic.

"Alphabet Soup had won the San Antonio Handicap earlier in the year. He just wouldn't let anyone by him," Hofmans said. "So I told Chris McCarron, who was riding him in the Breeders' Cup, that all I wanted him to do was get Alphabet Soup's head in front at some point."

McCarron had a willing partner. Alphabet Soup was in contention throughout, then went after the lead at the top of the stretch, with Cigar on his outside and Louis Quatorze just to his inside. And through a thrilling stretch run, he would not let either get past him.

"He was so determined," Hofmans said. "His ears were pinned back, just battling. I could see that Cigar was never going to get by him. He had his neck stretched out, and if you look at photos of the race, you can see he had his eye right on Cigar. But I didn't see Louis Quatorze on his inside. I thought he won by a long head, not a nostril."

Georgia Ridder, the owner of Alphabet Soup, is joined in the winner's circle by fellow Oak Tree Racing Association board member Sherwood Chillingworth (right), along with trainer David Hofmans and jockey Chris McCarron.

Did the Mounties get their man? Those who backed Alphabet Soup certainly did. They were reflecting in glory (below) after Alphabet Soup paid $41.70. Whether in Canadian or American dollars, that's a nice price. The victory was a popular one in Southern California, where Alphabet Soup was based, because it was seen as a reward for his owner, Georgia Ridder of Pasadena, who maintained a high-class racing stable for years following the death of her husband, newspaper magnate Ben Ridder. Alphabet Soup set a Woodbine track record of 2:01 for 1 1/4 miles. "He was the type of horse that even when you thought he was in high gear, he always had a little more to give you," said winning jockey Chris McCarron.

1996 Breeders' Cup lapel pin.

Hold all tickets. It's a photo finish. Epitome (above left, number 6) rallied boldly to catch Jeanne Jones in the 1987 Breeders' Cup Juvenile Fillies at Hollywood Park. The Phil Hauswald-trained filly paid $62.80, and put a big smile on the face of Benny Bell Williams, daughter of co-owner John A. Bell III. Proud Truth (below left) beat the masked man, Gate Dancer, in the last strides of the 1985 Breeders' Cup Classic at Aqueduct. Jorge Velasquez rode the winner for trainer John Veitch and the Darby Dan Farm of owner John Galbreath. That Classic marked the second straight tough-luck Breeders' Cup loss for Gate Dancer, who was disqualified from second to third in the 1984 Classic at Hollywood Park. Allen Paulson's Escena and jockey Gary Stevens (right, inside rail) stole the 1998 Breeders' Cup Distaff at Churchill Downs. Left alone on the lead, Escena had just enough left to hold off the late run of Banshee Breeze (number 4) to win by a nose. That race proved pivotal, for Escena, who was trained by Bill Mott, and was named the Eclipse Award-winning older filly or mare that year.

Their accomplishments are sublime. On a championship day of racing, featuring elite horses and trainers, they have stood out, with performances so brilliant they are both breathtaking and awe-inspiring. Skip Away looked like a steam train when he charged out of the final turn, his gray legs churning like the wheels on a locomotive, en route to a six-length victory in the 1997 Breeders' Cup Classic at Hollywood Park. Inside Information turned the 1995 Distaff at Belmont Park into a rout, winning by 13 1/2 lengths, the largest margin in Breeders' Cup history. And among trainers, no one has won more money, run more horses, nor greeted more of them in the winner's circle, than D. Wayne Lukas. They have been among the most dominant figures in the Breeders' Cup.

WHITE KNIGHT

For four seasons, Skip Away graced American racing, as his owner, Carolyn Hine, and her husband, Sonny, Skip Away's trainer, took him all over the country. He was a champion at 3 and 4, and Horse of the Year at 5, with the Breeders' Cup playing a part in all three seasons.

The Hines wanted to run in the 1996 Breeders' Cup at Woodbine, where Skip Away had captured the Woodbine Million that fall. They earmarked $480,000 to supplement Skip Away to the Classic. But Sonny was hospitalized with kidney stones and could not train the colt. Disappointed, the Hines decided to pass, and watched as Cigar, whom Skip Away had defeated in the Jockey Club Gold Cup, narrowly lost to Alphabet Soup and Louis Quatorze. Still, Skip Away was voted the nation's champion 3-year-old colt.

The following year, Skip Away arrived at the Breeders' Cup with some questions. He had finished in the top three every time while racing in Florida, Maryland, Massachusetts, New Jersey, New York, and Texas, but had won just 3 of 10 starts. Horses such as Formal Gold and Gentlemen had defeated him during the year, but Skip Away was the most resilient of an outstanding group of older horses that year. By the Breeders' Cup, he was still going, while his main rivals had gone to the sidelines.

The Hines put up the $480,000 supplemental fee. Next to the $22,500 they paid for Skip Away as a 2-year-old in training, it was the best investment they ever made.

SKIP AWAY - 1997 Classic

It's a gray day. Skip Away looks like he was produced by the mist that enveloped Hollywood Park during a training session days before the 1997 Breeders' Cup Classic.

There was no doubting Skip Away's superiority that afternoon. He prompted a sharp early pace under jockey Mike Smith, took the lead heading into the final turn, and drew away powerfully with his high, loping action, keeping up a relentless pace his rivals could not match. He became the first supplemental entry to win the Classic since Wild Again in 1984. His victory was so lopsided that Skip Away wrested the Eclipse Award for champion older horse from Formal Gold and Gentlemen, and gave Carolyn Hine the Eclipse Award as champion owner. But Skip Away lost out on Horse of the Year to Favorite Trick, the undefeated Breeders' Cup Juvenile winner.

Skip Away was like a child to the Hines. Carolyn fell in love with Skip Away, and the feeling seemed mutual. Carolyn could be standing off to the side of the barn, but if Skip Away heard her voice, he would poke his gray head outside the stall, turn in that direction, and tilt his ears forward. "Mommy loves you," she would say.

"Skip has touched my heart. I truly love him," she

said. "He gives me an inner glow. He warms me up."

Skip Away won his first seven starts of 1998, extending his winning streak to nine. And after a third-place finish in the Jockey Club Gold Cup, he arrived at Churchill Downs for the Breeders' Cup, the final start in his racing career. It was a bittersweet time for the Hines.

"I've been crying for days," Carolyn said. "There's going to be a void when he's retired. I wish he could race until he turned all white and had a long, gray beard like Santa Claus."

Skip Away could not complete the fairy-tale ending, finishing sixth in the Classic. He retired with 18 wins in 38 starts, and earnings of $9,616,360, second only to Cigar. But the strength of his record throughout the year—coupled, no doubt, with the memory of his overpowering victory in the Classic the previous year—at last placed the crown for Horse of the Year atop Skip Away's head.

The familiar blue shadow rolls worn by runners trained by Bob Baffert (below) dominated the 1998 Juvenile Fillies at Churchill Downs (right), when Silverbulletday, number 6, and Excellent Meeting, number 7, finished one-two in an intramural squabble that determined that year's champion 2-year-old filly. Silverbulletday left the paddock (above) having won 5 of 6 starts that year, but her lone defeat had been against her stablemate.

Silverbulletday's victory completed a glorious year at Churchill Downs for her owner, Mike Pegram (above, with grandson, Gator). Six months before that year's Breeders' Cup, Pegram won the 1998 Kentucky Derby with Real Quiet, completing a dream come true for someone who grew up attending the races at Churchill Downs and Ellis Park. When Real Quiet went to the sidelines after the Belmont Stakes, Silverbulletday came to the fore that summer and fall for Pegram and Baffert, who are best friends. Pegram, a successful businessman who plays as hard as he works, named Silverbulletday (below) after the nickname of his favorite beer. You can be sure Pegram and his pals made it a Silver Bullet day after the Breeders' Cup.

SOMEWHERE OVER THE RAINBOW

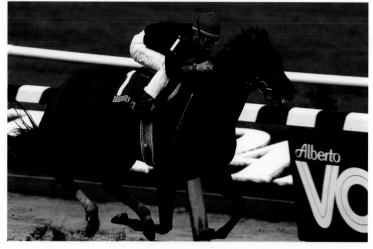

Throughout 1995, Shug McGaughey had employed a strategy of divide and conquer. The trainer was blessed with two outstanding 4-year-old fillies from the Phipps family—Heavenly Prize and Inside Information—and kept them apart all year long, winning stakes all over the Eastern portion of the United States.

Heavenly Prize, the champion 3-year-old filly of 1994, had in 1995 won the Apple Blossom, Go For Wand, Hempstead, and John A. Morris—all Grade I races—for her owner, Ogden Phipps. Inside Information, owned by Phipps' son, Dinny, had captured the Ruffian, Shuvee, and Spinster. On Breeders' Cup day at Belmont Park, they finally met.

The Phipps-owned entry was sent off at 4-5 against eight rivals, including that year's champion 3-year-old filly, Serena's Song. "Inside Information had won a hard-fought race in Kentucky in the Spinster, and we were concerned what that might have taken out of her," McGaughey remembered. Though both fillies were top-class, Heavenly Prize was regarded as the slightly better of the two. But the track that day was muddy.

"Heavenly Prize never liked an off track. Inside Information did, but in the back of my mind, I wondered, How good is she?" McGaughey said. "We found out."

Inside Information was spectacular. Despite breaking poorly, she rushed up to vie for the lead, took

over after a half-mile, and proceeded to pour it on. She was in front by six lengths with a furlong to go, and more than doubled that margin by the wire, winning by 13 1/2 lengths, a Breeders' Cup record. Her time of 1:46 for 1 1/8 miles was only three-fifths of a second off the track record. She had won her 14th race in 17 starts, and an Eclipse Award as the nation's best older filly or mare.

And as Inside Information awaited to head into the winner's circle, the sun peeked through the dark clouds, producing a glorious rainbow that framed the backstretch at Belmont Park.

"Inside Information overcame quite a few things," McGaughey said. "As a 3-year-old in the spring in Florida, she bruised a foot something terrible. Later that year, she had a pinched vertebrae in her neck. When we'd take her out to graze, she'd get spasms in her back legs. Once we got the inflammation out of her neck, she never missed a beat, but it was scary."

"How good is she? We found out."

The attention to detail paid by trainer Shug McGaughey (above) to Inside Information paid off when the filly, who overcame several physical ailments, romped through the mud under jockey Mike Smith in the 1995 Breeders' Cup Distaff (right). Inside Information, like another great McGaughey-trained filly, Personal Ensign, was by the sire Private Account.

INSIDE INFORMATION - 1995 Distaff

As a stablemate of Favorite Trick, the 1997 Horse of the Year, Countess Diana raced in his shadow all year long. But the champion 2-year-old filly of that year had a terrific season in her own right. She won 5 of 6 starts for trainer Pat Byrne, including this 8 1/2-length romp in the Breeders' Cup Juvenile Fillies at Hollywood Park. Among those she defeated were Beautiful Pleasure, who two years later won the Breeders' Cup Distaff at Gulfstream Park. Countess Diana, who was owned by Nancy and Richard Kaster and Nancy and Donald Propson, provided her jockey, Shane Sellers, with his first Breeders' Cup victory.

MEADOW STAR - 1990 Juvenile Fillies

There is no such thing as a sure thing, but bettors at Belmont Park in 1990 thought Meadow Star was close. The blaze-faced filly (left) was sent off as the 1-5 favorite against 12 rivals in the Breeders' Cup Juvenile Fillies. The price is a record for the shortest in Breeders' Cup history. Meadow Star lived up to expectations. Eighth early, she rallied wide on the turn, blew past her rivals, and drew off under jockey Jose Santos to win by five lengths, completing a perfect 7-for-7 season. LeRoy Jolley, who won the 1980 Kentucky Derby with the filly Genuine Risk, trained Meadow Star for owner Carl Icahn, who announced prior to the race that he would donate the filly's earnings to the Children's Rescue Fund, an organization that aids under-privileged children.

GILDED TIME - 1992 Juvenile

No one doubted the talent of Gilded Time (right), who entered the 1992 Breeders' Cup Juvenile at Gulfstream Park with a perfect record of three wins in three starts. But his ability to stretch out to two turns, and 1 1/16 miles, was a hurdle he had to clear. And he did, with help from jockey Chris McCarron. Gilded Time was difficult to handle early in the race, but McCarron, wearing the checkerboard red and white silks of owners David Milch and Jack and Marc Silverman, eventually got him to settle, enabling Gilded Time to hold off the late rush of It'sali'lknownfact. The victory marked the first in a Breeders' Cup race for trainer Darrell Vienna. Milch, a noted television producer, hit it big again the next year when "NYPD Blue" debuted.

BROCCO - 1993 Juvenile

The name is Brocco, Just Brocco. Albert Broccoli oversaw one of the greatest movie franchises of all-time as producer of the James Bond series. As a racehorse owner, Broccoli had several stakes winners, but his best horse was the one he named after himself. Brocco (left) was unbeaten in two starts heading into the 1993 Breeders' Cup Juvenile at Santa Anita. All eyes were on the unbeaten Eastern sensation Dehere, who that summer had swept Saratoga's three-race series for 2-year-old colts. But Dehere never fired, finishing eighth, while Brocco left his rivals shaken and the crowd stirred. Looking like a thunderbolt, the Randy Winick-trained colt won in a five-length blowout under jockey Gary Stevens.

DANCE SMARTLY - 1991 Distaff

All she wants to do is dance. In 1991, Dance Smartly won the Canadian Triple Crown. Sure, that's a great achievement, but it was made all the more remarkable considering that this was a 3-year-old filly beating the boys in three straight races, on both dirt and turf. For good measure, she beat them one more time, in the Molson Export Million. That fall, Dance Smartly (right) took on older fillies and mares in the Breeders' Cup Distaff at Churchill Downs. Along with entrymate Wilderness Song—both owned by Ernie Samuel's Sam-Son Farm and trained by Jim Day—they were sent off as the 1-2 favorite against 11 rivals. With Pat Day aboard, Dance Smartly completed her brilliant season with a clear-cut victory that made her 8-for-8 that year, and earned the Canadian-bred the Eclipse Award as the champion 3-

Artax had the need for speed. The Ernie Paragallo-owned colt set or equalled four track records during 1999, including this front-running victory in the Breeders' Cup Sprint at Gulfstream Park. But Artax might best be remembered for nimbly dodging an inebriated patron who wandered onto the track at Pimlico during a race on the 1999 Preakness undercard. The fan took a swing at Artax, but Artax eluded him and avoided a catastrophe. Louis Albertrani took over as the trainer of Artax early in the year, and guided him to a spectacular fall campaign. Artax closed the year by winning three straight races, his performances so dazzling that he became a finalist for Horse of the Year. Artax's regular rider was Jorge Chavez, who won his first two Breeders' Cup races on the 1999 card. Those victories helped propel Chavez, a native of Peru, to his first Eclipse Award as the nation's champion jockey.

Lukas, Lukas, Lukas. In the 1988 Breeders' Cup Juvenile Fillies at Churchill Downs, trainer D. Wayne Lukas sent out five runners and won led three of them—Open Mind, Darby Shuffle, and Lea Lucinda—sweep the best three spots. Open Mind was one of three Lukas-trained Breeders' Cup winners that afternoon.

RUNAWAY TRAINER

The Breeders' Cup numbers put up by trainer D. Wayne Lukas simply dwarf the rest of his brethren. Through 1999, Lukas had 126 starters, three times that of anyone else. He had won 15 races, twice as many as anyone else. And his runners had earned more than $15 million. No one else had hit the $10-million mark.

"After the Triple Crown, we point for the Breeders' Cup," Lukas said. "It's our second season."

Lukas won three Breeders' Cup races in 1988, and five times—in 1985, 1986, 1987, 1994, and 1999—won a pair of races. With five wins in the Juvenile, and four more in the Juvenile Fillies, he has been the dominant force in 2-year-old races.

Lukas's greatest day was in 1988 at Churchill Downs. Gulch rallied to capture the Sprint, and then a half-hour later, Open Mind led a 1-2-3 Lukas finish in the Juvenile Fillies. Later that day, Is It True upset heavily favored Easy Goer in the Juvenile. Lukas barely missed a fourth victory, when Winning Colors was nailed in the last jump of the Distaff by Personal Ensign. And Lukas finished second in the Mile with Steinlen.

"Without a doubt, the 1988 Breeders' Cup was our best single day of racing," Lukas said. "When you have that level of quality of trainers, jockeys, and horses, and you run in six races, win three, and come within an inch of winning a fourth, it's satisfying."

Lukas was content with the victories by Gulch and Open Mind, but when Is It True conquered Easy Goer, Lukas literally leaped with joy.

"Easy Goer was supposed to be the mortal lock of the 20th Century," Lukas said. "When Is It True won, I hopped over a rail that was about four-feet high—I was a lot younger then—and jogged down the chute. I was so happy."

OPEN MIND - 1988 Juvenile Fillies

In 1986, Lady's Secret clinched Horse of the Year with her victory in the Distaff at Santa Anita. She was tiny, but mighty.

"As a yearling, she wasn't much to look at," Lukas recalled. "She was this gray, little, ratty filly. And she never weighed more than 900 pounds. But she danced every dance.

"The key for her in 1986 was winning the Whitney," Lukas said. "She stepped outside her division and beat colts. When we won the Distaff, we had to wait for the Classic. Sure enough, the Horse of the Year candidates in that race stubbed their toe. She was the one who came through under pressure."

Flanders might have been Lukas's bravest winner. Despite suffering a career-ending injury in the 1994 Juvenile Fillies at Churchill Downs, she outbattled stablemate Serena's Song to win by a head. "With 2-year-olds, you never know which ones will go on, stand the test of time," Lukas said. "Serena's Song went on to be one of the all-time greats. Looking back, what Flanders did was unbelievable."

In 1999 at Gulfstream Park, Lukas scored upsets with Cash Run in the Juvenile Fillies, and Cat Thief in the Classic. Cash Run beat stablemate Surfside, the first foal out of Flanders.

Cat Thief had won just 1 of 11 starts in 1999 prior to the Classic, and had been beaten by several of the horses pointing for the race. His owner, W.T. Young, called together his advisers at Overbrook Farm to discuss whether to run in the Classic. Lukas and Young wanted to do it. Five others said no. "The vote was unanimous—two to five," Young said later.

Cat Thief came through, running the best race of

Trainer D. Wayne Lukas's pony, Spud (above), was Clint Eastwood's ghostly steed from the movie, "Pale Rider."

his career to hold off Budroyale and Golden Missile in a thrilling stretch drive. He provided Lukas, who has few missing spaces on his resume, with his first victory in the Classic.

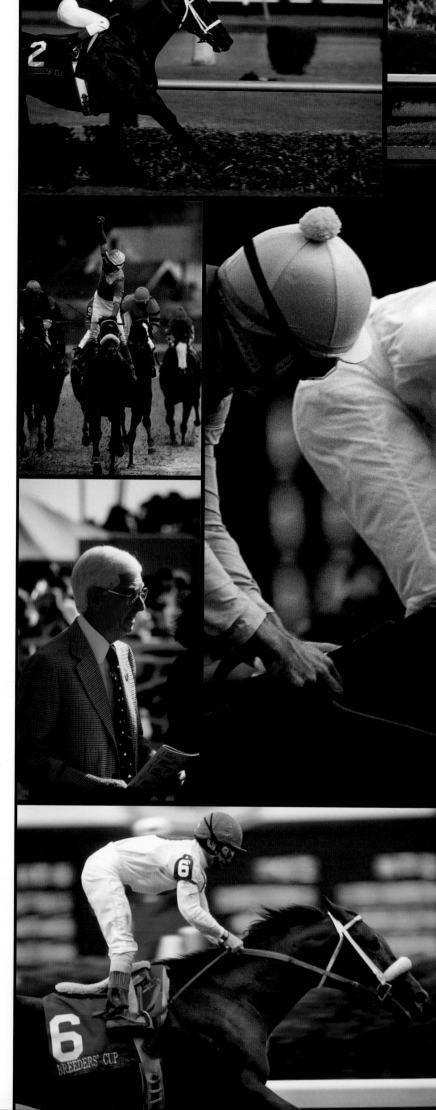

FLANDERS - 1994 Juvenile Fillies

How good was Flanders? No one can say for sure, due to an abbreviated career, but her defeated rival, Serena's Song, went on to become the all-time leading female money winner with career earnings of $3,283,388.

The white bridles worn by horses trained by D. Wayne Lukas have won more Breeders' Cup races than any other stable. Flanders, shown holding off barnmate Serena's Song in a thrilling Breeders' Cup Juvenile Fillies in 1994, is surrounded by a host of images reflecting Lukas's success in the Breeders' Cup. Clockwise from upper left are Breeders' Cup winners Steinlen, Cash Run, and Success Express, owner Gene Klein and his filly Lady's Secret, Boston Harbor, Cat Thief, Capote, Timber Country, owner W.T. Young of Overbrook Farm, and Gulch.

Jorge Chavez (right) comes from a destitute background. He was the product of a broken home, and was out on the streets, trying to survive, before he was a teenager. One day a friend suggested that the small boy try his luck as a jockey at the racetrack since he was so little. The course of his life was changed. After becoming the champion in his native Peru, Chavez did the same in the United States. Victories aboard Beautiful Pleasure and Artax in the 1999 Breeders' Cup earned him the Eclipse Award.

BEAUTIFUL PLEASURE - 1999 Distaff

Beautiful Pleasure (left) was carefully managed throughout 1999 by John Ward, Jr., and his wife, Donna. John was listed as the trainer, but he deferred credit to Donna, who was the regular exercise rider for Beautiful Pleasure. Donna's mission was to teach the high-strung filly to relax early in her races. The lessons were learned by Breeders' Cup Championship day. Wearing the colors of owner John Oxley, Beautiful Pleasure went right to the front in the Distaff, and never looked back.

1999 Breeders' Cup admission ticket.

Princess Rooney just missed earning an Eclipse Award in both 1982 and 1983. At age 4, in 1984, the Breeders' Cup provided her with a chance to erase that blemish. She was pointed all year for the inaugural Championship day at Hollywood Park, but in the week leading up to it, trainer Neil Drysdale (left) gave serious thought to running her in the Classic, against males, instead of the Distaff. Not wanting to risk losing the Eclipse Award again, Drysdale and the filly's owner, Paula Tucker, eventually decided to run in the Distaff. Lucky Lucky Lucky had her head in front as the field came past the stands the first time, but Princess Rooney's jockey, Eddie Delahoussaye, was merely waiting to turn loose the great gray filly. It was a mismatch. Princess Rooney won by seven lengths (below). How might she have done in the Classic? Her time for the 1 1/4 miles was a full second faster than Wild Again's. The Distaff marked Princess Rooney's career finale. She was a win machine, with 17 victories in 21 starts.

PRINCESS ROONEY · 1984 DISTAFF

WARRIORS

They are the horses we admire most. Tough, determined, and downright brilliant, they are possessed of an intense will to win, and the desire to come back for more year after year without losing their enthusiasm for racing, nor their ability to compete against top-class company. From a horse who overcame myriad physical problems to win the same race off a near two-year layoff, to a filly and a mare whose Hall of Fame careers were marred by the tragedy accompanying their lone meeting, these are some of the greatest warriors the Breeders' Cup has seen.

AN ALLURING COLT

Shug McGaughey had always thought highly of Lure, but it was not until the summer of the colt's 3-year-old year that his potential was unlocked by his trainer. "What's the matter with Lure?" Seth Hancock, whose Claiborne Farm owned Lure, asked McGaughey one morning. "I don't know," McGaughey replied.

A few days later, McGaughey, seeking to find the key to the son of Danzig, ran Lure in an allowance race on turf at Saratoga. His winning time left onlookers awestruck.

"Horses just don't do that this time of year," McGaughey's friend, handicapper Paul Cornman, told him after the race. A turf specialist had been born. Lure became a Breeders' Cup perennial, competing in three consecutive Championships, winning twice.

His specialty was the Mile. The great filly Miesque had won the Mile in successive years in 1987 and 1988. Lure matched her record. He scored victories in 1992 at Gulfstream Park, and 1993 at Santa Anita, utilizing the same front-running tactics each year. Each time, he won by daylight. No one could keep pace with him early, and no one could threaten him in the stretch run.

Yet as good as Lure was, he was born the wrong year. Despite his great record on the turf in 1992 and 1993, he missed out on an Eclipse Award each year.

Lure was one of the most accomplished turf runners of the 1990s. He retired with 14 victories in 25 starts, with nine of those victories coming in stakes races on the grass.

Lure began his Breeders' Cup career in 1992 at Gulfstream Park. He looked magnificent as he left the paddock that afternoon (opposite page) and headed out to the racetrack. "He was as good as any horse I've ever run," recalled his trainer, Shug McGaughey. "His coat glistened. He did make quite a presence in the paddock that day. It was hot, and he liked it hot." Lure sizzled in the 87-degree heat. Breaking from the inside post, and wearing saddle cloth number 2, he roared to the front and kept on rolling (below), covering one mile in 1:32 4/5 to set a course record. He also brought his jubilant breeder and owner, Seth Hancock (right, with wife Debbie), his first Breeders' Cup victory.

1992 Breeders' Cup admission tickets.

LURE - 1992 Mile

In 1993, Lure headed west, to Santa Anita, and again found conditions to his liking. It was 84 degrees on Championship day. Lure thrived in his training (above) but trainer Shug McGaughey gasped when he drew post 12 in the field of 13. With a short run to the first turn, McGaughey was concerned Lure would be caught wide. "When he drew the outside post, everybody said you can't win from there," McGaughey said. He and jockey Mike Smith came up with a plan. They decided to leave the gate aggressively. That was the winning move. As Lure sped away from the gate and set out after the lead, a brutal traffic jam behind him and to his inside eliminated several top contenders. Lure cruised along on the front end and drew off (right) to a 2 1/4 length victory.

LURE – 1993 Mile

Mike Smith (below) calls Lure one of the best horses he has ridden. But even a horse of Lure's stature could not pull off the unprecedented feat of winning three straight Breeders' Cup races. Lure tried for the hat trick in 1994 at Churchill Downs. But he had an unsightly tendon, then developed a quarter crack, and drew the outside post in a field of 14. The good fortune that had followed him the two previous years was running out. In what was to be his final race, Lure finished ninth. "We were hoping against hope," McGaughey said. "In two weeks, he would have been fine, but we did not have that option."

DA HOSS - 1996 Mile

The day before the 1996 Breeders' Cup Mile, trainer Michael Dickinson and his partner, Joan Wakefield, walked the turf course at Woodbine, seeking the best ground. They drew up a map, and gave it to Gary Stevens, who was to ride Da Hoss. Stevens, in red silks, followed the map to the buried treasure. After saving ground for the first six furlongs, Da Hoss came just one path off the rail for the stretch run, and kicked clear (opposite page).

DA HOSS

Da Hoss probably should have been a steeplechase runner, considering how many hurdles he had to clear. His physical problems were apparent early. As a yearling in 1993, he sold for just $6,000, the cheapest price that year for a son of Gone West. He was offered for sale to several parties at the end of his 2-year-old year, but, despite his promising race record, most veterinarians warned prospective clients off of him.

Da Hoss had troubles with his feet and his hocks, but the Preston brothers—Jack, Art, and J.R.—decided they would gamble. They purchased an 85-percent interest in Da Hoss, and embarked on a thrill ride that culminated in one of the most emotionally stirring stories in Breeders' Cup history.

The Preston brothers turned Da Hoss over to trainer Michael Dickinson at the beginning of his 3-year-old season. It was the perfect marriage. Da Hoss needed intensive monitoring, and the meticulous Dickinson was the ideal caretaker.

Dickinson guided Da Hoss to an accomplished 3-year-old year, including victories in the Del Mar Invitational Derby and the Jersey Derby. He was supposed to run in the Breeders' Cup Mile that year at Belmont Park, but rain earlier in the week had left the course deep. Dickinson, concerned the soft ground could harm Da Hoss, instead raced him in the Sprint. Da Hoss finished last in the field of 13.

One year later, at Woodbine in Toronto, Da Hoss was back, and this time in the Mile. Despite winning 2 of 4 starts that year, he had been hampered by soreness in his hind end. By October, though, he was in excellent condition, and he beat the best turf milers in the world.

His old injuries always presented problems, and as he aged, Da Hoss also had trouble with his tendons and fetlocks. He never made it to the races at age 5. The next year, Da Hoss several times was close to a race. Each time, though, he started to get sore, and Dickinson had to back off. Da Hoss's physical condition improved in the fall, and Dickinson began dreaming the impossible dream.

Dickinson had an audacious plan. He wanted to bring Da Hoss into the 1998 Mile off a two-year layoff, without a prep race. But, fearing the Breeders' Cup selection committee would relegate Da Hoss deep onto the list of also-eligibles for what was surely going to be an over-subscribed field, Dickinson realized Da Hoss would have to have one showcase start.

Races in mid-October at the Meadowlands and Belmont Park were rained out, so Da Hoss was sent to Virginia's Colonial Downs, where he won an allowance race.

Could a horse, hampered by numerous injuries and limited to just one start in two years, beat the best turf milers in the world? Sounds like a three-hankie tear-jerker in the movie theater. The crowd of 80,452 at Churchill Downs for the 1998 Breeders' Cup Mile doubted there would be a Hollywood ending, however, and sent Da Hoss off at 11-1. But Da Hoss was ready for the test. He moved up menacingly on the final turn, and took the lead after turning into the stretch.

At mid-stretch, however, Hawksley Hill and jockey Alex Solis edged past Da Hoss. Hawksley Hill put his head in front, and appeared headed for victory. But Da Hoss, driven by an innate desire embodied by the most courageous Thoroughbreds, bravely re-rallied under jockey John Velazquez to win by a head.

Trainer Michael Dickinson (left) was overcome with emotion, and cried tears of joy in the winner's circle, after Da Hoss won the Breeders' Cup Mile for the second time (above). "That day at Woodbine," he said, referring to Da Hoss's victory in the 1996 Breeders' Cup Mile, "was the happiest day of my life, but now this is. It's been an emotional roller coaster." Da Hoss, fittingly, never raced again. This victory was the perfect closing scene to his inspiring career.

ELMHURST - 1997 Sprint

When Elmhurst first arrived in this country, he had raced 17 times. And lost 17 times. Hardly the resume, one would think, of a Breeders' Cup winner. But Elmhurst, transformed into a brilliant, late-running sprinter by trainer Jenine Sahadi, (below) rallied from last to first in a 14-horse field to capture the 1997 Breeders' Cup Sprint at Hollywood Park. Elmhurst was following in the footsteps of his sire, Wild Again, who won the inaugural Breeders' Cup Classic at Hollywood Park in 1984. For Sahadi, owners Carol and C.N. Ray, and jockey Corey Nakatani, it was their second straight victory in the Sprint, having taken the 1996 version at Woodbine with another European-raced import, Lit de Justice.

PRECISIONIST

Few horses were as fast, versatile, or talented as Precisionist, who was quick enough to win going seven furlongs, yet had enough stamina to win going 1 1/4 miles, as he showed when sweeping Santa Anita's three-race Strub Series during the winter of 1985. But that summer at Hollywood Park, he bruised his feet after the Hollywood Gold Cup, and went to the sidelines.

His trainer, Ross Fenstermaker, knew if Precisionist was going to make that year's Breeders' Cup at Aqueduct, the only race he could possibly point for was the Sprint. It would be his first start in 4 1/2 months, and he would have to shorten up to six furlongs against the premier sprint specialists in the world.

That was a far cry from the previous year, when Precisionist tried to stretch his speed to 1 1/4 miles. Precisionist was one of the leading 3-year-olds of 1984. In the fall, he finished second in the Super Derby to Gate Dancer, then was seventh in the inaugural Breeders' Cup Classic at Hollywood Park. Now, he was being asked to turn back the clock and show the speed he had as a precocious 2-year-old.

Precisionist cooperated with the grand plan. He trained sensationally coming into the Sprint and was the third choice, at 3-1. He got a perfect trip and ride from Chris McCarron. Precisionist stalked the pace of Mt. Livermore and Smile, was tipped three paths wide for the stretch drive, and wore down Smile to win by three-quarters of a length in 1:08 2/5, just one-fifth of a second off the track record. He gave his 87-year-old owner, Fred Hooper, his first Breeders' Cup victory.

Precisionist finished third in the 1986 Classic at Santa Anita, then, after standing at stud in 1987, returned to race as a 7-year-old in 1988. He set a track record for one mile that summer at Del Mar and finished a game fifth in the Breeders' Cup Sprint at Churchill Downs.

Precisionist raced 46 times, and is one of just three horses to have made four starts in the Breeders' Cup, a warrior if there ever was one.

PRECISIONIST - 1985 Sprint

Precisionist's engine always was on overdrive. Even in the paddock (above) his neck was arched, and he was tugging at the bit, as if he could not wait to be let loose. Precisionist usually ran in middle-distance races, whose purse money, year-round, is better than that offered sprinters. But the 1985 Breeders' Cup Sprint (right) gave trainer Ross Fenstermaker a rare chance to show off Precisionist's speed. "He had that horse so primed for that race," winning rider Chris McCarron (number 3) said. "And you couldn't help but have confidence in Precisionist, because he tried so hard all the time."

After finishing second in the 1985 Breeders' Cup Sprint at Aqueduct (below), Smile returned in 1986 at Santa Anita (right), and sped to an 11-1 upset under jockey Jacinto Vasquez. The victory was crucial for Smile in his being voted the Eclipse Award as champion sprinter that year. Scotty Schulhofer trained Smile for Frances Genter, who four years later would win the Kentucky Derby with Unbridled.

THEATRICAL (Ire) – 1987 Turf

Theatrical kept trying until he got it right. He was 14th in the 1985 Breeders' Cup Turf, and second in 1986. In 1987, he was moved to the barn of trainer Bill Mott, who doubled (right) as Theatrical's exercise rider. The attention to detail paid off in that year's Breeders' Cup Turf at Hollywood Park (below), when Theatrical (number 2B) defeated the heralded European standout Trempolino, who was coming off a victory in France's prestigious Prix de l'Arc de Triomphe. Pat Day rode Theatrical for owner Allen Paulson, who bought out partner Bert Firestone on the eve of the race.

PASEANA (Arg) - 1992 Distaff

In her 1992 Breeders' Cup Distaff appearance, Paseana (left) galloped to a four-length victory at Gulfstream Park. Someone attempted to "hand" it to Paseana, as evidenced by an obvious handprint on her right hip (above). Paseana was trained by Ron McAnally, who had great Breeders' Cup success with another Argentine import, Bayakoa. Chris McCarron rode Paseana for owner Sid Craig, the husband of noted weight-loss executive Jenny Craig. Paseana tried to emulate Bayakoa as a two-time Breeders' Cup winner, but she lost the 1993 Distaff by a nose to Hollywood Wildcat.

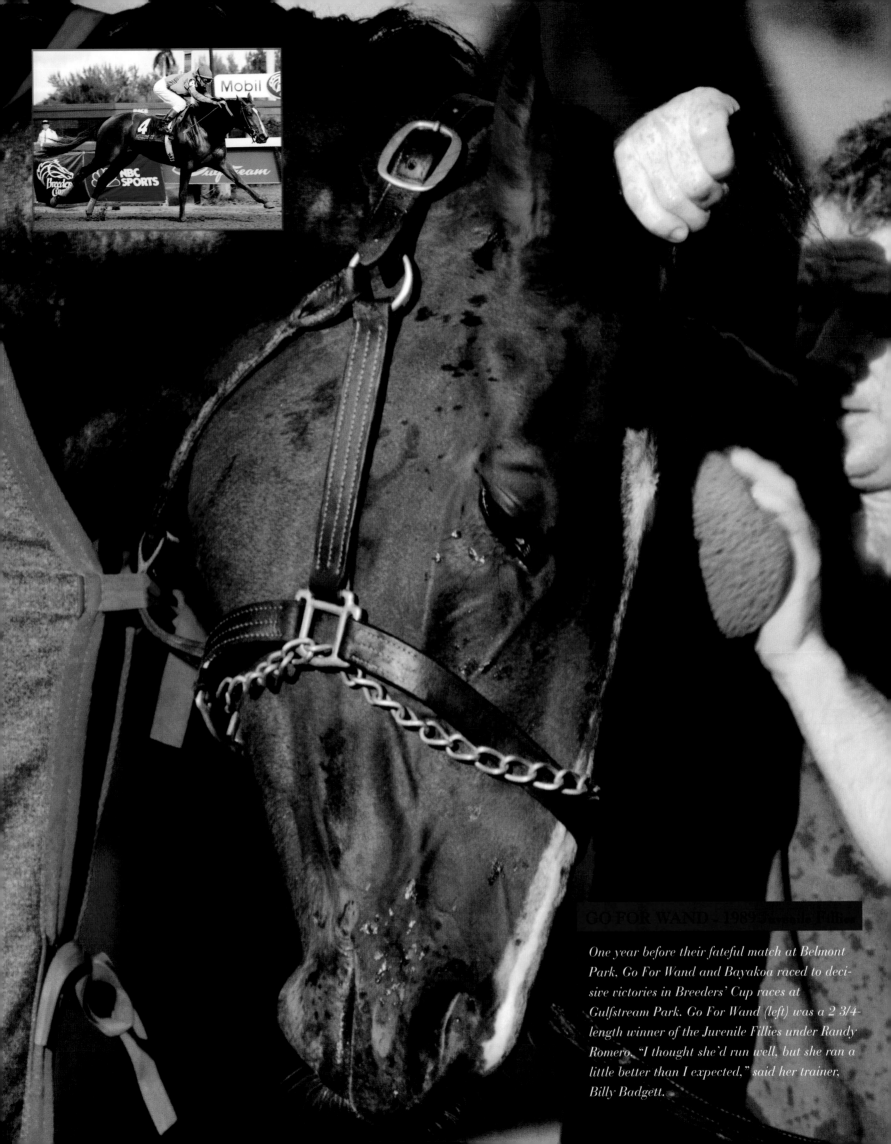

GO FOR WAND · 1989 Juvenile Fillies

One year before their fateful match at Belmont Park, Go For Wand and Bayakoa raced to decisive victories in Breeders' Cup races at Gulfstream Park. Go For Wand (left) was a 2 3/4-length winner of the Juvenile Fillies under Randy Romero. "I thought she'd run well, but she ran a little better than I expected," said her trainer, Billy Badgett.

LINKED IN TRIUMPH AND TRAGEDY

Go For Wand won the 1989 Juvenile Fillies at Gulfstream Park exactly 33 minutes before Bayakoa won the Distaff. By the next year, with both so clearly dominant in their divisions, the future Hall of Famers finally met in the Distaff at Belmont Park.

Both had been declared champions in 1989. "At that point, I didn't know how good she'd be," said Billy Badgett, who trained Go For Wand. She was plenty good. Go For Wand was unquestionably the leading 3-year-old filly in the country in 1990. She came into the Breeders' Cup with seven wins in eight starts that year, and was a candidate for Horse of the Year.

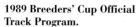

1989 Breeders' Cup Official Track Program.

Bayakoa, a nervous Argentine import who was soothed by the patient training of Ron McAnally, had taken a leap forward in the 1989 Distaff. Pressured by a tag-team from the barn of D. Wayne Lukas, she avoided a meltdown and turned back all challengers. The next year, Bayakoa again was the best older mare in the country. She came into the Breeders' Cup with six wins in nine starts, but was 6 for 7 against females; two of the losses came against males.

Go For Wand and Bayakoa were owned by great supporters of the sport. Jane du Pont Lunger's Christiana Stable, which owned Go For Wand, had raced classy horses since 1937. Frank and Jan Whitham, far newer to racing but just as desirous of a first-rate show, displayed their sportsmanship by twice paying a stiff supplemental fee of $200,000 to make Bayakoa eligible for the Distaff.

BAYAKOA (Arg) - 1989 Distaff

No one could keep up with Bayakoa (below), who used her speed to take the Distaff with Laffit Pincay, Jr. aboard. Bayakoa proved difficult to catch more often than not. The native of Argentina won 21 of 39 starts and was a champion both in South America and North America.

For the first mile of the 1 1/8-mile race, the 1990 Distaff was one of the greatest races of all time. Bayakoa and Go For Wand were locked together, unwavering, as they drew clear of their five rivals.

"It was a dogfight from the time they left the gate," Badgett said. "It was a pretty incredible race — until she got hurt."

With the two side by side, Go For Wand suddenly broke her right front ankle and fell. "It happened so quickly, I couldn't tell if it was us or the other filly," McAnally said. Bayakoa galloped alone to the finish line before an audience stunned into silence.

"I was happy that I had won, but it was a bad scene," said Laffit Pincay, Jr., who rode Bayakoa to both Breeders' Cup victories. "I could tell the other filly was hurt. It's hard to celebrate. I had mixed feelings."

Bayakoa had become a rare, two-time Breeders' Cup winner, but McAnally took no joy.

"I can't cope with something like this," he said that day. "I feel terrible. God bless Go For Wand. That's all I can say."

Go For Wand was buried the next day, at Saratoga Race Course. Bayakoa raced three more times. She never won another race.

BAYAKOA (Arg) – 1990 Distaff

Bayakoa (left) and Go For Wand (right) were virtually inseparable as they turned into the stretch of the 1990 Breeders' Cup Distaff at Belmont Park, just moments before Go For Wand's tragic accident. Go For Wand's jockey, Randy Romero (below left), was thrown clear of the stricken filly, but was injured and attended to by medical personnel. Go For Wand's death left fans in shock, and served as a sobering reminder of the fragility of the Thoroughbred.

SHOCKERS

The quality of the horses competing in the Breeders' Cup races is so deep that, inevitably, horses with accomplished race records still go off at astronomical odds. And the Breeders' Cup, while crowning champions, has not been immune to exposing the flaws of some of the best horses to have ever graced its stage. Be it a victory by a horse with a bad back, making his first start on dirt, his odds so large they could not fit on the tote board, or the defeat of a colt whose coronation seemed assured, these are some of the biggest upsets in Breeders' Cup history.

FRENCH KISS

In 1993, Jerry Bailey was starting to gather momentum toward his induction into the Hall of Fame two years later. He had won his first Breeders' Cup Classic in 1991, and earlier in 1993 had won his first Kentucky Derby, with Sea Hero. He was used to getting on some of the best horses in the country, and winning the biggest

races, but he had just four mounts in the 1993 Breeders' Cup, two of whom were rank longshots.

Bailey was 0 for 3 that day at Santa Anita when he arrived in the paddock for the Classic. He knew little about his mount. Two weeks earlier, Bailey did not even think he was going to ride in the race. His prospective mounts were alternates in what was surely going to be an overflow field. But, at the last moment, Bailey picked up the mount on a French import, Arcangues, when the jockey originally scheduled to ride that horse, Mike Smith, instead opted for Devil His Due.

The Classic field drew the best older runners from both East and West. Bobby Frankel had a three-ply entry headed by Bertrando, the Woodward Stakes winner, and Marquetry, who had won the Meadowlands Cup. California's favorite son, Best Pal, was supplemented to the Classic after winning the Goodwood Handicap three weeks earlier. Colonial Affair, the Belmont Stakes winner, Wallenda, who had won the Super Derby, and Miner's

ARCANGUES - 1993 Classic

The tote board can only display odds as high as 99-1, so no one knew what the exact price was on Arcangues as he flashed past the board, en route to a $269.20 payoff, the biggest upset in Breeders' Cup history.

Mark, already a winner against older horses in the Jockey Club Gold Cup, were three of the six 3-year-olds in the 13-horse field.

Bailey did not know what Arcangues's trainer, Andre Fabre, nor his owner, Daniel Wildenstein, looked like. He had never seen the horse. So he went to a spot in the paddock where it appeared the number 11 horse would stop, and awaited the call of "riders up."

"Some kid with the horse threw me up on him and started talking to me in French," Bailey remembered. "I just nodded my head. I had no idea what he was saying. Now I know what the Spanish guys do when they come to this country and don't know English."

As the horses were going through the tunnel to the racetrack, Fabre hurriedly ran beside Arcangues and shouted instructions to Bailey, but the din in the tunnel drowned out his voice.

"I just figured, 'He's a European, he'll probably drop out of it and finish,'" Bailey said. "Then I looked at the board and saw he was 99-1. I thought, 'I hope he doesn't come jogging in an eighth of a mile behind .'"

Arcangues never had raced on dirt, and had been bothered throughout his career by a bad back. Fabre brought him to the Breeders' Cup with the Classic in mind, believing the level surfaces of American dirt courses would better suit Arcangues's aches and pains. But Bailey

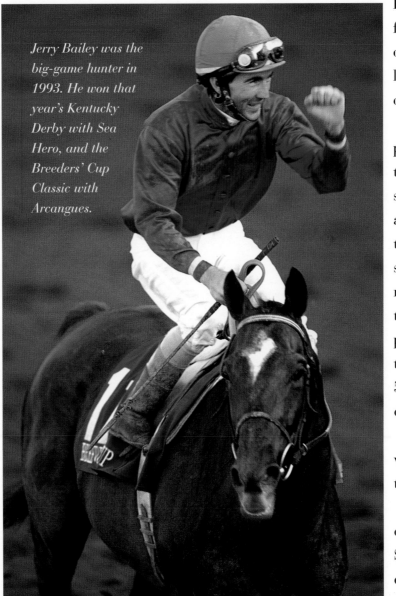

Jerry Bailey was the big-game hunter in 1993. He won that year's Kentucky Derby with Sea Hero, and the Breeders' Cup Classic with Arcangues.

knew none of that.

"I warmed him up and he felt great, and from the time he broke out of the gate, he was on the bridle," Bailey said. "As we turned up the backside, there was a horse in front of me, Ezzoud, who was going well, so I just thought I'd stay on the rail and follow him. When you're on a longshot, nobody's looking for you, so you can take more risks."

Arcangues started passing rivals on the far turn, then accelerated strongly between Ezzoud and Bertrando after turning into the homestretch. In an instant, he roared past Bertrando, then drew off to an emphatic two-length victory. The crowd of 55,130 was stunned in disbelief.

"I'm sure everybody was saying, 'Who's that?'" Bailey said.

Arcangues had gone off at 133-1, and paid $269.20 to win, the largest win payoff in Breeders' Cup history.

"As the years have gone by, so many people have told me they bet Arcangues," Bailey said. "If all those people had bet him, he wouldn't have paid $269.

"It was a strange race to win because I had no history with the horse, and at the time, I hadn't developed a relationship with Fabre or the Wildensteins. It was like a one-night stand. It turned out pretty good for me. It'll probably never happen again, but it was great that time."

OUTSTANDINGLY - 1984 Juvenile Fillies

LASHKARI (GB) – 1984 Turf

The inaugural Breeders' Cup Turf was supposed to be a showcase for the nation's most popular horse, John Henry, but he was injured a week before the race, leaving a wide-open field for the $2-million race. The field included a Kentucky Derby winner in Gato Del Sol, a Horse of the Year in All Along, and a globetrotting, international star in Strawberry Road. But it was the unheralded Lashkari (below), wearing the dark green silks of The Aga Khan, who stormed down the course to post the upset (opposite page). The winner's share of the purse was $900,000. Laskhari had made $57,903 in his previous seven starts combined.

THE TRENDSETTER

There might not have been an Arcangues, nor the great participation of Europeans over the years, had foreigners not fared well in the first Breeders' Cup. It was not unusual in 1984 for Europeans to come to the United States for important races, such as the Washington D.C. International, but the Breeders' Cup extended their season deeper into the calendar year, and there was doubt that Europeans could hold their form as late as November 10, let alone reproduce that form following a transatlantic trip.

Yet five of the 11 runners in the inaugural Breeders' Cup Turf came from Europe that fall, two directly, three with intermediate stops in North America. The last to arrive was Lashkari, who had won a stakes race at Longchamp less than three weeks before the Breeders' Cup. Ten days before the Breeders' Cup, his trainer, Alain de Royer-Dupre, who had never run a horse in North

America, and owner, The Aga Khan, decided to send Lashkari to Hollywood Park. Lashkari arrived on Wednesday, and was not released from quarantine until Friday. Less than 24 hours later, he broke from the gate in the Turf.

Knowledge of European form was not as sophisticated then as it is now. Lashkari had won 3 of 7 starts in Europe, and was ridden by Yves Saint-Martin, a 15-time champion in his native France. Yet Lashkari was ignored. He was the longest shot in the race, at 53-1.

Lashkari raced in midpack through the first mile of the 1 1/2-mile race, then came flying down the center of the course to catch All Along—whose dazzling North American invasion in 1983 earned her Horse of the Year honors—to win by a neck. Lashkari paid $108.80.

Lashkari did not win a championship, nor many friends among those who had backed shorter-priced horses that day. But he proved to skeptics that Europeans could win on Breeders' Cup Championship day.

The view must have looked good to trainer Bob Baffert (left) when he sent out Thirty Slews (above) to an 18-1 surprise in the 1992 Breeders' Cup Sprint at Gulfstream Park. With Eddie Delahoussaye up, Thirty Slews wore down pacesetter Meafara in the final yards to claim the victory for a partnership that included owners Mitch Degroot and Mike Pegram. That win was the first on a national stage for Baffert, but before the decade was out, he had established himself as one of the sport's leaders. In the 1990s, Baffert twice won the Kentucky Derby and Preakness Stakes, and three times was voted the Eclipse Award as champion trainer.

1992 Breeders' Cup event pin.

Owner Madeleine Paulson (right) and jockey Pat Valenzuela (below) were all smiles after 14-1 shot Fraise (bottom) sneaked through along the rail to upset odds-on favorite Sky Classic in the 1992 Breeders' Cup Turf at Gulfstream Park.

Paulson acquired Fraise after winning a golf bet from her husband, Allen, who earlier on that Breeders' Cup card had won the Juvenile Fillies with Eliza. Valenzuela rode both Eliza and Fraise. Fraise, bred by Allen Paulson and trained by Bill Mott, numbered three Grade I wins among his ten lifetime victories.

CAT THIEF - 1999 Classic

When 19-1 shot Cat Thief (white blinkers), 26-1 longshot Budroyale (second from left), and 75-1 outsider Golden Missile (far left) ran 1-2-3 in the 1999 Breeders' Cup Classic at Gulfstream Park, they produced the highest trifecta payoff in Breeders' Cup history, $39,031.20 for a $2 wager. Cat Thief, owned by W.T. Young's Overbrook Farm, was ridden by Pat Day. His trainer was D. Wayne Lukas, who put his stamp on Cat Thief right between the eyes.

Tom Proctor was a lonely man the week of the 1994 Breeders' Cup. The 38-year-old trainer had longshot One Dreamer in the Distaff. And no one wanted to talk to him. Reporters at Churchill Downs trudged past his barn to talk to the trainers of Heavenly Prize, Hollywood Wildcat, and Sky Beauty, all of whom went off at 2-1 or less and were expected to dominate the race.

"Don't you want to talk to me?" Proctor would playfully yell as another reporter marched by, oblivious.

They all wanted to talk to him at 2:33 on Saturday afternoon. One Dreamer, dismissed at 47-1, led from start to finish under Gary Stevens and held on to win by

a neck over Heavenly Prize, paying $96.20. Hollywood Wildcat was sixth, and Sky Beauty last, in the field of nine.

"She had won earlier in the year at Churchill Downs, so right then we pointed for the Distaff," Proctor said. "I thought she had a shot. But win? Things like that don't happen to me. I had a good time all week. There was no pressure. No one knew we were there. I bet a little, because I wanted to have a little party in case she won. I had to party for two months to spend it all."

As One Dreamer left the track, her exercise rider, Pete Garrett, walked alongside, his long ponytail flapping as he animatedly bowed to the crowd.

"He did what I felt like doing," Proctor said. "It would have taken two butterfly nets to catch Pete."

ONE DREAMER - 1994 Distaff

One Dreamer was in the same spot the first time by the stands (opposite page) as she was at the end of the race (below) in the 1994 Breeders' Cup Distaff. With Heavenly Prize bearing down on her from the outside, One Dreamer had just enough left to prevail. One Dreamer was owned and bred by the Glen Hill Farm of Leonard Lavin, the chairman of the board of Alberto-Culver, a long-time sponsor of the Breeders' Cup.

Bravo, bravo. Pete Garrett, the exercise rider for One Dreamer, accepted congratulations for the mare from fans lining the outer rail at Churchill Downs following her $96.20 upset.

Miss Alleged (below) was given so little chance of winning the 1991 Breeders' Cup Turf at Churchill Downs that she was assigned to the mutuel field. The track linemaker believed that she and two others had the least chance of winning. She sure looked overmatched on paper. Miss Alleged had lost all six of her previous starts that year while racing in France. But she blossomed in North America. In the Breeders' Cup, she wore down Itsallgreektome in the final strides (left) to win at odds of 42-1 under jockey Eric Legrix. A few weeks later, she beat the boys again in the Hollywood Turf Cup. In another upset, those two victories made Miss Alleged the Eclipse Award winner as champion female turf horse for owner Issam Fares's Fares Farm Inc.

1991 Breeders' Cup pin.

Three times earlier in 1988, Is It True had lost to Easy Goer. So when both colts went into the gate for that year's Breeders' Cup Juvenile, Laffit Pincay, Jr., riding Is It True, had no reason to believe the outcome would be different in Round Four.

"We were going further," Pincay said. "Easy Goer, I thought, was almost unbeatable."

Easy Goer was the most talked-about 2-year-old since Secretariat. The robust son of Alydar had blazed through New York's juvenile stakes scene in the summer and fall, and arrived in Kentucky as the clear leader of his division. He was 3-10, at the time the shortest price in Breeders' Cup history.

Churchill Downs, however, proved to be Easy Goer's Achilles heel. In a race that eerily foretold of the trouble Easy Goer would have on a similar muddy track six months later in the Kentucky Derby, the front-running Is It True held on to beat Easy Goer by 1 1/4 lengths, despite running the final five-sixteenths of a mile in a dawdling 34 2/5 seconds.

"I thought he was going to give up, but he kept on going," Pincay said. "I felt Easy Goer coming, so I came out a little. When he felt Easy Goer coming, he gave me a little more."

Laffit Pincay, Jr. (above) was skeptical of his chances of beating Easy Goer with his mount, Is It True. "When he went to the lead on the backside," Pincay said, "I didn't know if he was going to last or not." But Is It True surprised him, and the fans who had made Easy Goer the favorite, by holding off Easy Goer (below) to win at odds of 9-1 for trainer D. Wayne Lukas and owner Gene Klein.

OPENING VERSE – 1991 Mile

With so many top horses competing in each Breeders' Cup race, there are bound to be generous prices on horses who get over-looked. Pat Valenzuela guided Opening Verse (right) to a $55.40 stunner in the 1991 Mile at Churchill Downs. A half-hour later, Valenzuela, again wearing the red, white, and blue silks of owner Allen Paulson, rode Arazi to his unforgettable victory in the Juvenile.

ANEES – 1999 Juvenile

Anees (left) was last midway through the 1999 Juvenile at Gulfstream Park, but he passed all 13 of his rivals with a powerful stretch kick to win, paying $62.60. Anees, ridden by Gary Stevens for Prince Ahmed Salman's The Thoroughbred Corporation, was the second Breeders' Cup winner for trainer Alex Hassinger, Jr., who also took the 1992 Juvenile Fillies with Eliza.

VERY SUBTLE – 1987 Sprint

Fillies have done exceptionally well in the Sprint, but none has been as dazzling as Very Subtle (right), who embarrassed a top field in 1987 at Hollywood Park, winning by four lengths under Pat Valenzuela and paying $34.80. The 3-year-old filly beat such talented older males as Groovy, who still was named the year's champion sprinter despite finishing second as the odds-on favorite. Mel Stute trained Very Subtle for Ben Rochelle.

DESERT STORMER – 1995 Sprint

Joanne Nor's homebred Desert Stormer (left), trained by Frank Lyons, returned $31 when she beat the boys in the 1995 Sprint at Belmont Park. She probably would have paid three times that had she not been coupled with two other horses as part of the mutuel field. She and jockey Kent Desormeaux beat Mr. Greeley and jockey Julie Krone by a neck.

TOP TEN
BREEDERS' CUP
LONGSHOTS

1. Arcangues
$269.20
1993 Classic
Santa Anita Park

2. Lashkari (GB)
$108.80
1984 Turf
Hollywood Park

3. One Dreamer
$96.20
1994 Distaff
Churchill Downs

4. Miss Alleged
$86.20
1991 Turf
Churchill Downs

5. Last Tycoon (Ire)
$75.80
1986 Mile
Santa Anita Park

6. Cash Run
$67.00
1999 Juvenile Fillies
Gulfstream Park

7. Wild Again
$64.60
1984 Classic
Hollywood Park

8. Epitome
$62.80
1987 Juvenile Fillies
Hollywood Park

ACROSS
THE
POND

From the beginning, the Breeders' Cup was designed to showcase not only the best horses in North America, but the best in the world, too. The task of getting horses to come from Europe was thought difficult, since the Breeders' Cup would be scheduled approximately one month after the major championship races in Europe. Foreign horses would have to ship across the ocean, and try and hold their form against horses who had been pointed specifically for the Breeders' Cup. But the allure of millions of dollars, plus the simple, noble concept of sportsmanship, has compelled owners and trainers of foreign horses to compete in every Breeders' Cup race, not just the turf races, but those on dirt, too. The very best have covered their countries, and the Breeders' Cup, in glory.

THE DUBAI BROTHERS

The Maktoum brothers, the rulers of Dubai in the United Arab Emirates, have campaigned horses all over the world. Their participation has evolved from merely buying horses at Kentucky yearling sales 20 years ago to setting up modern, full-scale racing and training facilities in their native land. Horses who spend the winter in Dubai, then head out to conquer the world, compete in the royal blue silks of Godolphin Racing, named for the Godolphin Arabian, one of the three founding sires of the modern Thoroughbred.

No horse has better exemplified the lofty, international ideals of Godolphin than Daylami. He raced on three continents in 1999, won Group I races in England and Ireland, and completed his career with a breathtaking victory in that year's Breeders' Cup Turf.

Daylami was the best horse in Europe that summer, when he won the King George VI and Queen Elizabeth Stakes by five lengths, and the Irish Champion Stakes by nine. But he struggled on a heavy, tiring course in the Prix de l'Arc de Triomphe and finished ninth, 23 1/2 lengths behind Montjeu.

Immediately after the race, it appeared Daylami would be retired. But Sheikh Mohammed al Maktoum, the

Jockey Frankie Dettori reaches down to hug trainer Saeed bin Suroor (above) after Daylami's stirring performance in the 1999 Breeders' Cup Turf at Gulfstream Park. The victory was so impressive that Eclipse Award voters made Daylami a finalist for Horse of the Year, even though that was Daylami's lone start in this country that year. Dettori was so happy (below) that he jumped for joy.

driving force behind Godolphin, and trainer Saeed bin Suroor reconsidered, and decided to head to Gulfstream Park for the Breeders' Cup.

In two previous Breeders' Cups in Florida, European horses had been shut out. The theory was that the warm weather in Florida sapped the strength of the Europeans, who already were growing their winter coats because brisk, fall weather had arrived overseas. Gulfstream's tight turns and firm turf also were thought to be factors.

Daylami, however, overcame all those obstacles. He arrived in Florida three weeks before the Breeders' Cup, giving him plenty of time to acclimate. And then he went out and turned in the day's best effort. With a stirring stretch kick, Daylami roared past Royal Anthem and Buck's Boy, who had won the Breeders' Cup Turf in 1998, and cruised home 2 1/2 lengths in front to stamp himself the best turf horse in the world.

Though Sheikh Mohammed had won previous Breeders' Cup races, Daylami's victory was the first under the Godolphin banner. No one believes it will be the last.

The victory was sweet redemption for Daylami's jockey, Frankie Dettori, who had been roundly and justifiably criticized the previous year for an ill-conceived ride aboard Swain in the Breeders' Cup Classic at Churchill Downs. When Dettori arrived in the winner's circle (left), a wide smile creasing his face, he yelled, "What about Swain? What about Swain?"

Dettori then leaped animatedly from Daylami's back, his joy magnified by the great relief he felt.

"For 12 months, I've been carrying this on my shoulders," he said. Daylami's victory was the biggest win in the U.S. for Sheikh Mohammed's (bottom) Godolphin Racing stable, yet another example of the far-reaching scope of this international powerhouse.

RIDGEWOOD PEARL (GB) - 1995 Mile

Irish eyes were smiling on the filly Ridgewood Pearl, who slogged her way through a soft, tiring turf course to beat the boys and the Americans in the 1995 Breeders' Cup Mile at Belmont Park (left). Nicknamed for Anne and Sean Coughlan, Ridgewood Pearl was trained by John Oxx.

The victory by Ridgewood Pearl set off a burst of patriotism among the Irish when jockey John Murtagh arrived in the winner's circle (right). The Breeders' Cup incorporated turf racing into its program to lure the best horses in the world, particularly from Europe, where top-class racing is conducted almost exclusively on grass. Brilliant fillies like Ridgewood Pearl have proven their quality on both sides of the Atlantic.

NORTHERN SPUR (Ire) - 1995 Turf

Northern Spur (number 11, left) had the luck of the Irish on his side. He was bred on the auld sod, was trained in the United States by Ron McAnally, and was ridden to victory in the 1995 Breeders' Cup Turf by Chris McCarron. Carnegie and Tamure, the third- and fourth-place finishers in that race, also were bred in Ireland. Northern Spur raced just four times in 1995 for owner Charles Cella. His Breeders' Cup victory proved crucial in his being named the champion turf horse in the U.S.

Hail Brittania! Journalist John McCririck has enlivened the Breeders' Cup with both his outrageous sartorial choices, and his brilliant handicapping predictions. Standard for McCririck are his cap, reading glasses, muttonchop sideburns, rings on each finger, and a fistful of tickets on whoever Frankie Dettori is riding.

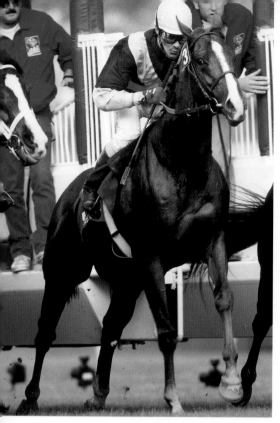

Spinning World finished second in the 1996 Breeders' Cup Mile at Woodbine to Da Hoss, then returned the following year and captured the 1997 Mile at Hollywood Park. Unlike most Europeans, he broke sharply (above), and when jockey Cash Asmussen asked him for his best, Spinning World grabbed the bit (right) and breezed past his rivals. Spinning World, owned by the Niarchos family's Flaxman Holdings, was trained by an exuberant Jonathan Pease (below).

Lester Piggott is to British racing what Bill Shoemaker is to American racing. He is the icon, the jockey to whom all are measured. Piggott ruled racing in Great Britain. He won the Epsom Derby nine times, and won 21 other classics.

Piggott retired in 1985 and became a trainer, but two years later was jailed after pleading guilty to charges of tax fraud. He was sentenced to three years in prison, but was paroled after one year. And in the fall of 1990, at age 54, he decided to return to race riding.

Shoemaker's favorite partner was Charlie Whittingham, considered one of the greatest trainers in the history of the sport. Piggott had a long association with the legendary Irish trainer Vincent O'Brien, who won 44 classic races, including six Epsom Derbies with horses such as Nijinsky, Roberto, Sir Ivor, and The Minstrel.

O'Brien was near the end of his career, and Piggott was trying to resurrect his, when they came to Belmont Park for the 1990 Breeders' Cup. They teamed in the Mile with Royal Academy, a son of Nijinsky.

Sent off the 5-2 favorite, Royal Academy was in 11th place in the 13-horse field during the early going. Piggott took Royal Academy to the middle of the turf course for the stretch run, and Royal Academy produced a powerful finish that enabled him to get up in the final strides and beat Itsallgreektome by a neck.

In the press box, pandemonium broke out. As the field charged down the stretch, cries of "Lester, Lester," rang out from the British press corps. When Royal Academy crossed the line first, British press members embraced one another with tear-filled hugs. The conquering hero had returned, writing another chapter to a glorious, yet star-crossed, career.

"Today," Piggott said, "is a dream come true."

Few races have been as emotionally draining as that of Lester Piggott aboard Royal Academy in the 1990 Breeders' Cup Mile at Belmont Park. Only 37 minutes earlier, Go For Wand had lost her life in a horrible accident in the Distaff. The crowd was reeling when Piggott left the paddock (opposite page). But when he came from far back to prevail in the final strides (below), his countrymen let loose with unrestrained shouts of joy. Royal Academy raced for Classic Thoroughbred PLC, a publicly-traded company on the Irish stock exchange.

ROYAL ACADEMY - 1990 Mile

Europeans are not supposed to be able to handle the dirt as well as Americans. And they certainly are not supposed to be able to sprint as quickly as the fastest Americans. But Hilal Salem's Sheikh Albadou crushed the Yanks at their favorite game (right), winning the 1991 Breeders' Cup Sprint at Churchill Downs by three lengths under jockey Pat Eddery (above). There were hugs all around (below) after Sheikh Albadou's 26-1 upset. But triumph turned to tragedy years later, when Sheikh Albadou's young trainer, Alex Scott, was tragically murdered by a disgruntled employee.

SHEIKH ALBADOU (GB) – 1991 Sprint

The brilliant French jockey Yves Saint-Martin fashioned one of the greatest rides in Breeders' Cup history when he guided Richard Strauss's Last Tycoon to a $73.80 surprise in the 1986 Breeders' Cup Mile at Santa Anita. Last Tycoon, trained by Robert Collet, was considered a sprinter, and he had not raced in more than two months. Saint-Martin saved every inch of ground until the top of the stretch, eased out for the stretch run, and kept Last Tycoon going through the demanding final yards to win by a head.

LAST TYCOON (Ire) – 1986 Mile

IN THE WINGS (GB) - 1990 Turf

Sometimes a European horse needs the guiding hands of an American jockey, familiar with the local courses, to get him home first. Sheikh Mohammed al Maktoum's In the Wings could only manage to finish fifth in the 1990 Prix de l'Arc de Triomphe, but three weeks later, with Gary Stevens riding him for the first time (above), he rallied to take the Breeders' Cup Turf at Belmont Park for trainer André Fabre. Tikkanen raced in France, Germany, Ireland, and Italy in 1994 for trainer Jonathan Pease and the Augustin Stable of owner George Strawbridge, but his greatest moment came in the U.S. in the Breeders' Cup Turf at Churchill Downs (below), when piloted by a rider with the all-American name of Mike Smith.

TIKKANEN - 1994 Turf

BARATHEA (Ire) - 1994 Mile

After Barathea bore out sharply on the first turn in the 1993 Breeders' Cup Mile at Santa Anita, trainer Luca Cumani made sure that would not happen in the 1994 Mile at Churchill Downs. Barathea was trained in England over a course designed to approximate the turns at Churchill Downs. In the race, he handled the turns flawlessly, and drew off for a three-length victory to give jockey Frankie Dettori his first Breeders' Cup win. Barathea was owned by Sheikh Mohammed al Maktoum and Gerald Leigh.

Jockey Walter Swinburn nearly was killed in a horrifying accident in Hong Kong at the beginning of 1996, so his victory aboard Lord Weinstock's Pilsudski (above and below) in that year's Breeders' Cup Turf at Woodbine left him near tears, appreciative for being able to compete, and to cradle a trophy from a Breeders' Cup win. Pilsudski, trained by Sir Michael Stoute, beat a star-studded field that included Singspiel, who won that year's Japan Cup. The next year, Pilsudski won the Japan Cup, too.

1996 VIP pin.

ROCK AND ROLL

You could not help but fall in love with Pebbles. Her trainer, Clive Brittain, treated her to a pint of Guinness stout a day. She listened to music on an oversized radio. She was adorable, a chestnut-colored filly with a big, white blaze cascading down her face. And she had a gelding for a boyfriend.

Pebbles was accompanied to the 1985 Breeders' Cup Turf at Aqueduct by Come on the Blues, a 6-year-old gelding whose sole responsibility at the Breeders' Cup was keeping Pebbles happy.

Pebbles, owned by Sheikh Mohammed, had captured the English 1,000 Guineas as a 3-year-old, and in 1985 was ranked as both the champion older filly and champion miler in England. But she was not an original nominee to the Breeders' Cup, and thus had to be supplemented for $240,000, 12 percent of the Turf's $2-million purse. It was money well spent.

The tight turns of Aqueduct's turf course caused

PEBBLES (GB) - 1985 Turf

Pebbles was an intelligent horse, inquisitive in new surroundings. When being walked each morning at Aqueduct, she often would look around, her ears pricked forward, swiveling like radar dishes.

the field to bunch at several points, notably on the final turn, when Pebbles was eager to run, but found her path blocked. Her jockey, Pat Eddery, waited patiently, hoping a hole would open, and was rewarded when Strawberry Road switched to the outside, leaving the rail for Pebbles.

Pebbles had wicked acceleration. She burst through the hole quickly and went from fourth to first within 100 yards, and had a one-length lead with a furlong to go. Strawberry Road, now racing in the middle of the course, made a belated run, but Pebbles had plenty left to hold him off and win by a neck.

Pebbles had set a course record for 1 1/2 miles, and had claimed a title in the U.S., too, for her one victory was good enough to get Pebbles an Eclipse Award as the nation's best female grass runner. Drinks all around.

Royal Heroine had a remarkably dramatic year in 1984, the Irish-bred filly's only full campaign in the United States after being imported from Europe. In March, she fell and was badly cut in a chain-reaction accident at Santa Anita that killed two mares. That summer, Royal Heroine stretched out to a mile and a quarter and beat everyone but the legendary John Henry in the Arlington Million. Shortened up for the inaugural Breeders' Cup Mile at Hollywood Park, the swaybacked filly trained sensationally for John Gosden, and was sent off as the favorite. With jockey Fernando Toro, who was wearing the internationally famed colors of owner Robert Sangster, Royal Heroine flew around the course in 1:32 3/5 to set both a course and an American record.

TWO TIMING LADY

Few foreign horses have had as much success, nor have left such a lasting impression, as did Miesque.

She ran twice in the United States, both times stepping out of her division to face males. She won the Breeders' Cup Mile in 1987 at Hollywood Park and earned the Eclipse Award as champion female turf runner. One year later, she returned and won the Mile at Churchill Downs, becoming the first two-time winner of a Breeders' Cup race and again earning a year-end championship off just the one start here. Later she was elected into the National Museum of Racing and

Hall of Fame in Saratoga Springs, New York.

Miesque was bred in the United States, but spent most of her career in France. She was bred and owned by Stavros Niarchos, a native of Greece who made a fortune in shipbuilding. She was trained by Francois Boutin, one of France's greatest trainers, and was ridden by Freddie Head, whose prominent French racing family included his father, legendary trainer Alec, and his sister, Criquette, a top trainer in her own right.

By the time Miesque arrived in California for the 1987 Breeders' Cup, she was an international star. She had already won six Group I races, and was the champion 2-

MIESQUE - 1987 Mile

Following in the footsteps of Royal Heroine three years earlier, Miesque set a record over Hollywood Park's newly enlarged turf course in the 1987 Breeders' Cup Mile. She was so far in front that jockey Freddie Head took her in hand and was gearing her down at the finish.

MIESQUE - 1988 Mile

Encore! Encore! Miesque wins the Breeders' Cup Mile for the second straight year, this time at Churchill Downs in 1988, becoming the first horse to win a Breeders' Cup race twice and in consecutive years. Her trainer, Francois Boutin (bottom), also won the 1991 Breeders' Cup Juvenile with Arazi.

year-old in France in 1986. And she was about to conquer America.

Miesque embarrassed the Mile field. Grass races are known for close, nail-biting finishes, yet Miesque blew away her rivals, winning by 3 1/2 lengths in 1:32 4/5, a course record.

The next year, Miesque had an abbreviated campaign, but it was every bit as glorious. She won twice in three starts in France, all in Group I company, before heading to Kentucky for what would be her final start. It was a homecoming of sorts, for Miesque had been born in the bluegrass near Lexington, and she would live there in retirement as a broodmare.

Again, it was no contest. Miesque humbled her 11 rivals, winning by four lengths on a course that had been softened by rain. The conditions were in stark contrast to the previous year, when Miesque won on a Hollywood Park course that was as firm as a billiard table.

Miesque could adapt to any situation: different countries, different courses, it did not matter. She won 12 of 16 starts, and never finished worse than third. *C'est magnifique.*

FABULOUS FIVE

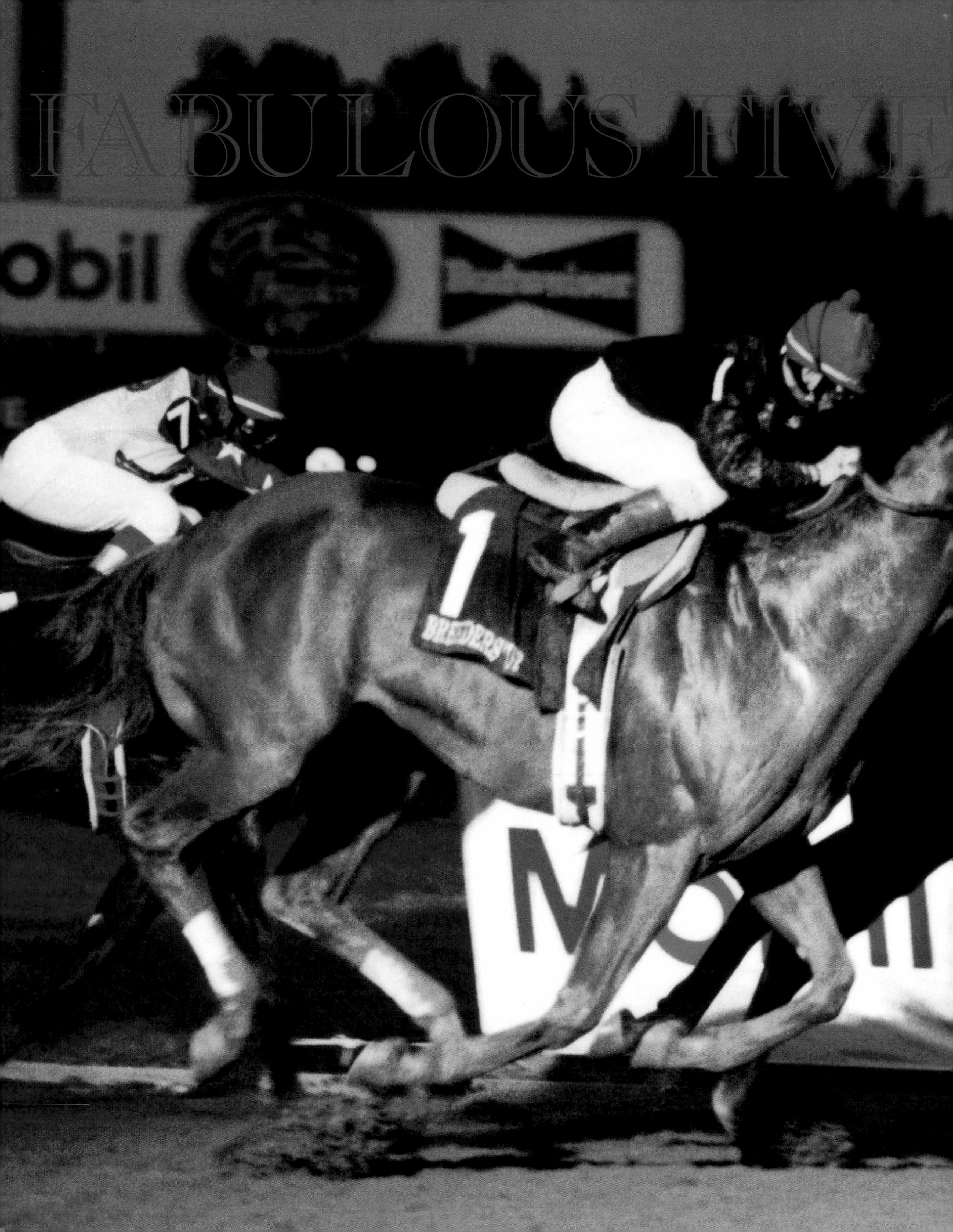

Whether it is the perfect game of Don Larsen in the World Series, or the dominance of Michael Jordan in carrying the Chicago Bulls to six National Basketball Association titles, every sport's championship has its signature moments, and players. The Breeders' Cup has been graced by racing's premier athletes, both human and equine, whose performances have stamped unforgettable memories onto the history pages of the sport. From the culmination of a thrilling, year-long rivalry between two Hall of Fame colts, to a filly whose courage and unwavering resolve allowed her to complete an unbeaten career, to a jockey who stands above his peers on Championship day, these are the moments that define the Breeders' Cup.

EAST IS EAST AND WEST IS BEST

The Dodgers vs. the Yankees. The Lakers vs. the Celtics. Some of the greatest rivalries in sports have matched teams from both coasts, whose fans support their heroes without question. In racing, the great rivalries matching the West against the East have included Swaps vs. Nashua, and Affirmed vs. Alydar. And in 1989, the Breeders' Cup provided the denouement for the last great rivalry of the century.

Sunday Silence and Easy Goer were born just a few furlongs from one another in central Kentucky, but by the time they got to the track, they had been claimed by the respective coasts on which they raced. Sunday Silence dominated the West Coast's preps for the Kentucky Derby, including an 11-length blowout in the Santa Anita Derby. Easy Goer was crushing his opposition in New York. Their Triple Crown was not only a battle between two great colts, but between two sets of rabid fans.

Sunday Silence won the Derby in the mud, a surface over which Easy Goer struggled. But in the Preakness Stakes two weeks later, Sunday Silence outdueled Easy Goer in a breathtaking, stretch-long drive. He was one race away from the Triple Crown.

The battle lines between East and West grew more defined, with fans and press from both coasts lauding their hero, and questioning the merits of the other. The feelings were not hiding below the surface; they were front and center. So much so that as Easy Goer came charging through the stretch with a clear lead in the Belmont Stakes—and was about to deny Sunday Silence the Triple Crown—the Belmont Park track announcer, Marshall Cassidy, called the leader "New York's Easy Goer."

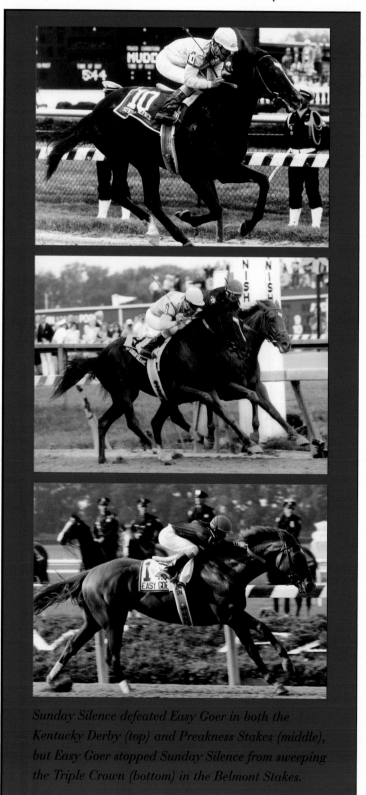

Sunday Silence defeated Easy Goer in both the Kentucky Derby (top) and Preakness Stakes (middle), but Easy Goer stopped Sunday Silence from sweeping the Triple Crown (bottom) in the Belmont Stakes.

Who was better? Sunday Silence had won two-thirds of the Triple Crown, but Easy Goer had pummeled him in the Belmont. The answer would come on Breeders' Cup day.

"It has been an amazing rivalry," said Shug McGaughey, the trainer of Easy Goer, "but it hasn't been one that lasted for just five weeks in the spring. It's gone on and on. Ever since Easy Goer beat Sunday Silence in the Belmont Stakes, people have been waiting for the fourth round."

The two colts didn't meet again until the Breeders' Cup Classic that year at Gulfstream Park. Sunday Silence and Easy Goer had dominated racing in 1989 to such an extent that there was no question that Horse of the Year honors were on the line.

"I've got to win to be Horse of the Year," said Charlie Whittingham, who trained Sunday Silence and owned him in partnership with Arthur Hancock III and Dr. Ernest Gaillard. "My horse comes up to the race perfect. As Trevor Denman says, 'You can go to the window.'"

There was anxiety in both camps. Less than two weeks before the Breeders' Cup, Pat Valenzuela, the regular rider for Sunday Silence, tested positive for cocaine and was given a 60-day suspension by stewards at Santa Anita's Oak Tree meeting. Chris McCarron picked up the mount. Whittingham tried to shrug it off. "There are a lot of top riders," he said. "You need the horse first. If you've got a bad horse, that's more of a problem."

Easy Goer was coming off a resounding victory against older horses in the Jockey Club Gold Cup, but was being bothered by sore ankles. He was the 1-2 favorite. Sunday Silence was 2-1. The third choice in the race, Western Playboy, was 16-1.

The day of the Breeders' Cup, around 5 a.m., both Sunday Silence and Easy Goer had a pre-race gallop. Unlike the bitterness harbored by some of the fans of both colts, Whittingham and McGaughey had grown close during the Triple Crown. And so had their stable hands. Pam Mabes, the exercise rider for Sunday Silence, was in the midst of her gallop when she noticed David Carroll, riding Easy Goer, right behind her. "Wanna race?" she said, playfully, as they galloped energetically through the homestretch.

Twelve hours later, the bell rang for Round Four.

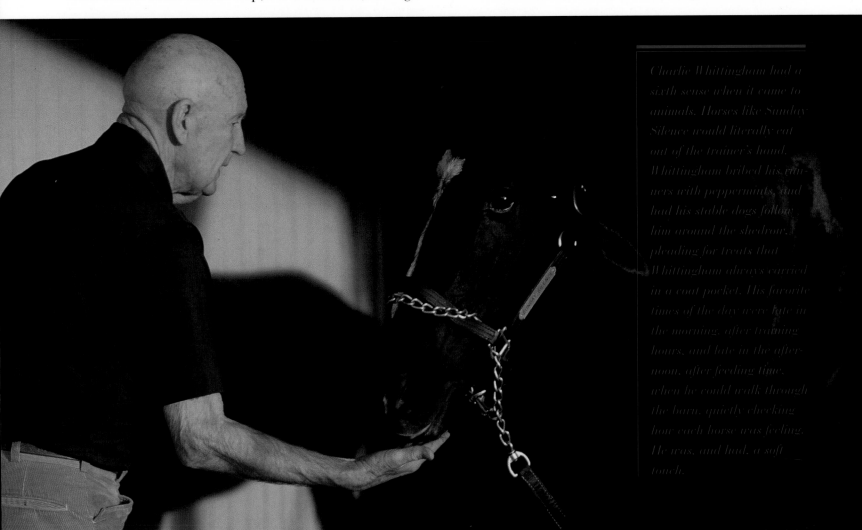

Charlie Whittingham had a sixth sense when it came to animals. Horses like Sunday Silence would literally eat out of the trainer's hand. Whittingham bribed his runners with peppermints, and had his stable dogs follow him around the shedrow, pleading for treats that Whittingham always carried in a coat pocket. His favorite times of the day were late in the morning, after training hours, and late in the afternoon, after feeding time, when he could walk through the barn, quietly checking how each horse was feeling. He was, and had, a soft touch.

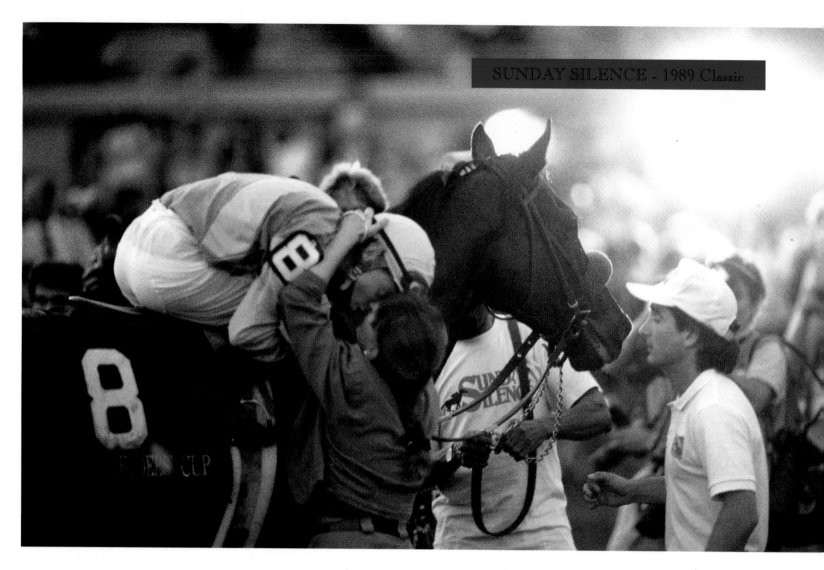

SUNDAY SILENCE - 1989 Classic

Easy Goer, breaking from the inside, took a stutter-step to his left leaving the gate and lost position. Sunday Silence, meanwhile, broke cleanly from the outside and settled into position just behind the early leaders. As the field neared the far turn, Sunday Silence crept closer to the front, and Easy Goer moved in, too. Easy Goer got within a half-length of Sunday Silence, but then they hit the turn, and Sunday Silence was gone.

"Sunday Silence was better on the turns than Easy Goer," McCarron said. "He was a length in front of him going into the turn, and four in front coming out of it. That's where the race was won."

Easy Goer tried to recover. After straightening away for the stretch run, he closed furiously. McCarron repeatedly looked over his right shoulder, both nervous and anxious. "Sunday Silence would wait on horses when he made the lead," McCarron said. "When he put Blushing

John away, I looked back and saw Easy Goer flying. Charlie said, 'Don't hit him with the whip, whatever you do.' I didn't. But I was tempted."

Sunday Silence held on to win by a neck. He had defeated Easy Goer three times in their four meetings, and had secured Horse of the Year. And in the end, fans of both Sunday Silence and Easy Goer had to concede admiration for their rival, for the presence of one colt always brought out the very best in the other.

Sunday Silence (above) was in the spotlight throughout 1989, but never more so than after clinching Horse of the Year with his Breeders' Cup Classic victory at Gulfstream Park.

1989 Breeders' Cup Official Track Program and admission ticket.

A PERFECT LADY

Personal Ensign was supposed to run in the Breeders' Cup for the first time in 1986, but the day before she was going to be sent to Santa Anita for the Juvenile Fillies, she fractured a hind pastern bone in a workout at Belmont Park, and underwent surgery.

"She needed five or six screws," said Shug McGaughey, who trained her for Ogden Phipps. "I thought we'd just save her to breed, but the surgeons said it wouldn't bother her to race."

It was two years later before Personal Ensign made it to the Breeders' Cup, but the wait was worth it, for she turned in the most dramatic, courageous performance in the event's history.

Personal Ensign came into the 1988 Breeders' Cup Distaff with a perfect 12-for-12 record. Not since the first decade of the century, when Colin won all 15 of his starts, had an American-based horse won that many races, without a defeat, against top-class company. It was announced before the race that the Distaff would be Personal Ensign's career finale. She was going to be a broodmare the following spring.

That summer, Personal Ensign had defeated males in the Whitney Handicap at Saratoga, one of five Grade I wins she had already earned that year. She was a candidate for Horse of the Year. And she was the 1-2 favorite against eight rivals in the Distaff.

But midway through the race, Personal Ensign was in trouble. She was struggling to keep up on the muddy Churchill Downs surface as Winning Colors, who six months earlier had won the Kentucky Derby in similar front-running fashion, skipped along uncontested on the lead. McGaughey turned to a friend and whispered, "Not today."

Despite the conditions, Personal Ensign kept plugging away. She was fifth at the top of the stretch, then third with a furlong to go, but was still four lengths behind Winning Colors.

Midway through the 1988 Breeders' Cup Distaff, Shug McGaughey (right), Personal Ensign's trainer, was pessimistic. "She didn't like the going, and she had two good fillies—Winning Colors and Goodbye Halo—in front of her," McGaughey remembered. "As the thing unfolded, I thought she was going home 12 for 13."

Ogden Phipps (left), who bred and owned Personal Ensign, has been a great supporter of racing at the highest level for decades. He and his son, Ogden Mills Phipps, breed and race horses from the finest bloodlines. Phipps has also won Breeders' Cup races with Dancing Spree and My Flag, all of them trained by Shug McGaughey.

The gray filly, Winning Colors, is desperately trying to hold on, but Personal Ensign (left) is wearing her down in the final strides of the long stretch at Churchill Downs.

There is, in all Thoroughbreds, a born desire to run. But only the very best have the will, stamped in them from birth, to fight through adversity and deliver their best every time. Personal Ensign was one of those rare racehorses, and the last furlong of her career was about to be a testament to her greatness.

She gained ground with every stride, inch by inch, but the wire was closing fast. Yet somehow, in those final 220 yards, Personal Ensign made up the difference, her nose reaching the wire an instant before Winning Colors.

When the photo finish sign came down, and Personal Ensign's number 6 was placed first on the toteboard, a roar went up from the crowd. Spontaneous cheering broke out, and scores of people dabbed at their eyes, emotionally overcome by what they had just witnessed.

"This is the greatest thrill of my life," said her jockey, Randy Romero. "I always dreamed of riding an undefeated horse. There's one in a million like her, and she's the one."

"It shows what a good filly she is to overcome the track," McGaughey said. "She's a very, very good filly with a lot of courage. I don't want to take anything away from anyone else, but I'm not sure how well she handled the track today. I thought she was beat. I didn't think she had a chance until the final five or six jumps. She's been very special to us."

Personal Ensign had a memorable career as a broodmare, too. In 1992, Ogden Phipps bred her to Easy Goer, and the following spring, Personal Ensign produced a filly. The filly was named My Flag (right), and in 1995 at Belmont Park, My Flag won the Juvenile Fillies, making Personal Ensign the first mare to win a Breeders' Cup race and then produce a Breeders' Cup winner. Like mother, like daughter, My Flag rallied from far back to win over a muddy track.

Deja vu. Personal Ensign (above left) and her daughter My Flag (above right, number 9) look like mirror images of one another winning their respective Breeders' Cup races. My Flag seemingly had two strikes against her when the track came up muddy for the 1995 Juvenile Fillies at Belmont Park. Her mother never was comfortable on an off track, and her father, Easy Goer, suffered two of the biggest losses of his career on wet tracks. But, in the case of My Flag, two negatives equalled a positive.

PERSONAL ENSIGN - 1988 Distaff

*Like Personal Ensign, the career of her jockey,
Randy Romero, was infused with great courage.
Romero was severely burned in an accident in a
hot box at Oaklawn Park in 1983, and broke just
about every bone in his body in a series of riding
accidents. But he willed himself to come back time
and time again. On Breeders' Cup Championship
day in 1988, Romero and Personal Ensign were
number one.*

Alysheba had his neck arched in the post parade, radiating power, like a powder keg about to explode. And once the race started, that power was unleashed. "He had a very abrupt turn of foot," said Chris McCarron, who rode Alysheba to his greatest victories.

AMERICA'S HORSE

Personal Ensign was not Horse of the Year, but only because one of the best, and most popular, horses in years completed a great career with a victory later that day in the Breeders' Cup Classic.

Alysheba won the Kentucky Derby and Preakness in 1987, then lost a narrow decision to Ferdinand in that year's Classic at Hollywood Park. Alysheba started 1988 by thumping Ferdinand twice at Santa Anita. The crown had been passed. Alysheba was the best male horse in the land.

Alysheba was the champion 3-year-old of 1987, and already was a lock as champion older horse of 1988. Now, he had returned to the site of his Derby victory, needing a win in the Classic to secure Horse of the Year.

A late post time, combined with the wet, dreary weather, left the track in near darkness by the time the Classic was run. Alysheba looked magnificent in the post parade, his neck arched proudly as he headed to the starting gate for what would be his final race.

The starting gate was barely visible from the grandstand. As the field came by the stands for the first time, flashbulbs popped like fireflies as fans tried to capture the moment. With Chris McCarron aboard, Alysheba settled just off the leaders in the early going, grabbed the lead at the top of the stretch, then turned back the challenge of Seeking the Gold in the final furlong.

"He has an incredible turn of foot," McCarron said. "I have to grab a hold of his mane before I ask him to run because his acceleration literally throws my balance off. You have to be ready for it.

"When Seeking the Gold ranged outside of me, I put Alysheba into a drive, and he did his thing," McCarron added. He had done it. He was Horse of the Year.

"It was a great relief," McCarron said. "He had a great following."

One fan near the winner's circle held up a sign that read, "Alysheba for President."

Seeing it, Van Berg said, "He's got my vote."

"People loved him. He had such charisma," Van Berg remembered.

"The pressure was on us after Personal Ensign won the Distaff," said Jack Van Berg (above), who trained Alysheba for owners Dorothy and Pamela Scharbauer. "I knew if Alysheba didn't win the Classic, she would have been Horse of the Year." Alysheba also was trying to win a Breeders' Cup race after two previous attempts. As a 2-year-old in 1986 (middle), he was a fast-finishing third with Bill Shoemaker in the Juvenile at Santa Anita. And in 1987 (bottom), he was nosed out by Ferdinand and, ironically, Shoemaker in the Classic at Hollywood Park.

ALYSHEBA - 1988 Classic

The bright lights for the photo finish camera sliced through the gloaming, acting as a spotlight as Alysheba crossed under the wire (left and above).

"That bright light looked like the entry to something," jockey Chris McCarron said. The Horse of the Year title, perhaps?

The victory, worth $1.35 million, pushed Alysheba's earnings to $6,679,242, which vaulted him past John Henry to become, at the time, the richest horse in history. John Henry, who competed until age 9, raced 83 times. Alysheba, who retired after the Classic, made 26 starts.

"The thing that impresses me the most about Alysheba is how quickly he accomplished what John did," said McCarron, who rode both horses. "Alysheba's the best horse I've ever ridden. No question."

No horse in Breeders' Cup history has made a better first impression than Arazi, whose electrifying victory in his American debut in the 1991 Juvenile might be the event's best individual performance. Arazi disappointed as a 3-year-old, which has dulled his legacy. But for one brief, shining, moment on a gorgeous afternoon at Churchill Downs, he was the most talked-about horse in the world.

Arazi arrived from France, where he was that country's champion 2-year-old colt. He had never run on dirt, and the hectic morning atmosphere at Churchill Downs the week before Breeders' Cup unnerved him. When he would go out to train, he would prop and wheel, frequently tossing Pat Valenzuela, his jockey.

Arazi's morning antics did not discourage Valenzuela. His confidence had been boosted by watching videotape of Arazi's races at the California home of the colt's owner, Allen Paulson.

"I went over to his house. We're sitting in the living room, and there's no TV," Valenzuela recalled. "Mr. Paulson hits a remote, and down comes this projection TV. The whole wall was like a screen."

"If you win the Breeders' Cup on this horse, you'll get a TV like this," Paulson told Valenzuela.

Valenzuela, however, was concerned when Arazi drew the outside post in the field of 14 in the 1 1/16-mile race. Valenzuela knew Arazi would have to be a superior racehorse to win.

"I wanted to get him to relax and save ground," Valenzuela recalled. "When we turned into the backstretch, he was in front of one horse. I wanted to move up a little. I smooched to him, and he took off."

Arazi grabbed a hold of the bit and was flying, careening through traffic like a motorist trying to evade the highway patrol. "Whenever he saw an open spot, he went right through it," Valenzuela said. "It was like playing a video game in an arcade." By the time the field reached the middle of the far turn, Arazi had gone from 13th to

second, with only Bertrando, the early leader, still in front of Arazi.

"Alex Solis was on Bertrando. When I got up to him, Alex looked over and did a double-take. I still had my feet on the dashboard," Valenzuela said. Arazi, racing well off the rail, ran past Bertrando effortlessly. He had gone from 13th to first in a half-mile, and showed no signs of slowing down.

Arazi opened a five-length lead at mid-stretch, and probably could have doubled that by the finish. But Valenzuela took hold of the reins nearing the wire and allowed Arazi to coast home five lengths in front.

"The next Kentucky Derby winner!" Valenzuela yelled, raising his whip in triumph as Arazi crossed the finish line. Arazi did not win the next year's Derby. But his place in Breeders' Cup history was secure.

Arazi was all alone as he and jockey Pat Valenzuela passed beneath the famed twin spires at Churchill Downs and headed to the finish line in the 1991 Breeders' Cup Juvenile. Arazi blew the race open on the far turn (opposite page), when he made a slingshot move and roared to the lead. He was moving so quickly that centrifugal force carried him to the middle of the track.

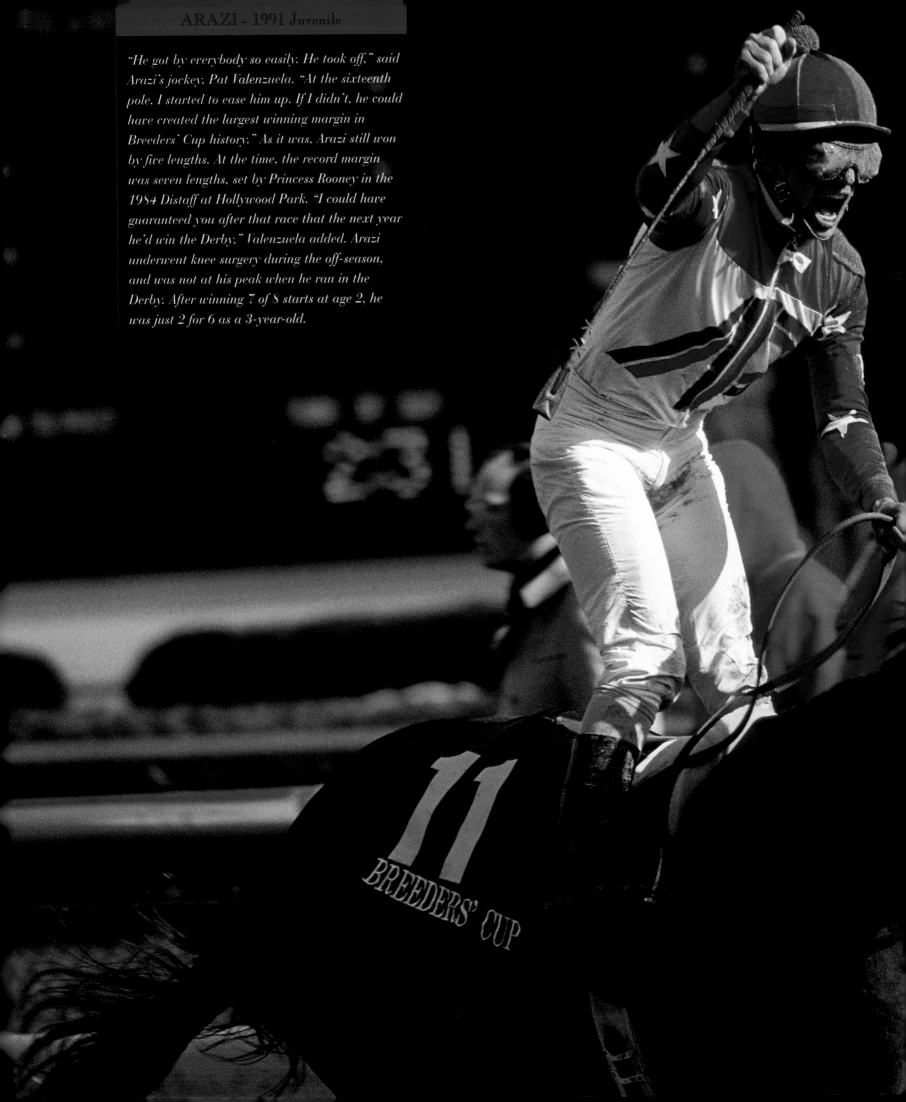

"He got by everybody so easily. He took off," said Arazi's jockey, Pat Valenzuela. "At the sixteenth pole, I started to ease him up. If I didn't, he could have created the largest winning margin in Breeders' Cup history." As it was, Arazi still won by five lengths. At the time, the record margin was seven lengths, set by Princess Rooney in the 1984 Distaff at Hollywood Park. "I could have guaranteed you after that race that the next year he'd win the Derby," Valenzuela added. Arazi underwent knee surgery during the off-season, and was not at his peak when he ran in the Derby. After winning 7 of 8 starts at age 2, he was just 2 for 6 as a 3-year-old.

LITTLE BIG MAN

Pat Day stands tall for someone who is not quite 5-feet in height. His posture is ramrod straight. He looks you right in the eye when engaged in conversation. He projects an aura of credibility and decency. He speaks with conviction, most passionately when it comes to his faith, which has been a guiding force in Day's life since 1984.

Perhaps it is a coincidence that 1984, the first year of the Breeders' Cup, marked a turning point in Day's life both personally and professionally. But Day does not believe in coincidences, saying, "I believe things are divinely orchestrated."

In January 1984, personal problems threatened to derail Day's career. On January 27, Day embraced his faith unwaveringly. "I gave serious consideration to getting out of racing," he said. "I was going to sell my equipment and go into the seminary. But the Lord told me to stay in racing."

That November, at the inaugural Breeders' Cup at Hollywood Park, Day captured the Classic with the longshot Wild Again after a tense, rough, stretch duel. He earned his first Eclipse Award as champion jockey, and saw his career blossom.

"I believe that race was instrumental in my getting the Eclipse Award," Day said. "That one single race took my career to the next level. I got national exposure, international exposure."

Day has been the dominant jockey in the Breeders' Cup ever since. Through 1999, he had won 11 races, and his mounts had earned nearly $20 million, both Breeders' Cup records among jockeys.

Day had won the Classic four times, with Wild Again, Unbridled (1990), Awesome Again (1998), and Cat Thief (1999). Victories on Favorite Trick in the 1997 Juvenile, and Lady's Secret in the 1986 Distaff, completed Horse of the Year campaigns. His other winners were Dance Smartly (1991 Distaff), Epitome (1987 Juvenile Fillies), Flanders (1994 Juvenile Fillies), Theatrical (1987 Turf), and Timber Country (1994 Juvenile).

Flanders was injured in the 1994 Juvenile Fillies and never ran again, but she has gone on to a successful career as a broodmare. Her first foal was Surfside, who finished third in the 1999 Juvenile Fillies. The courage displayed by Flanders that day, as she fought off her stablemate, Serena's Song, is recalled fondly by Day.

"She was incredibly gutsy," he said. "And with all that Serena's Song went on to do, it gets me thinking what Flanders could have done." Serena's Song was the champion 3-year-old filly the following year, and went on to become the all-time leading female money winner.

"She and Serena's Song were together from flagfall to the finish," Day said. "She was unbelievable."

Unbridled overcame the outside post position in a 14-horse field to win the Classic, but his victory was overshadowed by the death of Go For Wand earlier that afternoon at Belmont Park.

"It was a great ending to a dismal day," Day said. "When the filly broke down, a lot of us were ready to throw in the towel. We prayed in the jockeys' room. It was the saddest day in the history of the Breeders' Cup."

Always a crowd favorite, Pat Day didn't disappoint his fans when he rode Lady's Secret (above) to victory in the 1986 Breeders' Cup Distaff, or when he won the 1987 Breeders' Cup Turf on Theatrical (bottom right).

Awesome Again rallied from eighth at Churchill Downs to beat a field that included Silver Charm, Victory Gallop, Coronado's Quest, Skip Away, Touch Gold, Gentlemen, and European star Swain.

"Of all my Breeders' Cup wins, that was the most satisfying, because of the depth of the field. It might have been the best field ever assembled anywhere, certainly for a Breeders' Cup race," Day said.

"At the head of the stretch, I anticipated having to come around Silver Charm and Swain. But Swain drifted out, so I thought I'd split him and Silver Charm. Then Gary Stevens came out with Silver Charm, following Swain. So, I ended up with a straight shot down the center of the racetrack."

Cat Thief pulled off a 19-1 upset at Gulfstream Park. "That was very sweet, because he'd been a bridesmaid a time or two," Day said. "He had a killer instinct that day. He showed a tendency to be wimpy in his races earlier in the year."

Did Day ever think, back in 1984, that he would be the Breeders' Cup's leading jockey?

"Absolutely not," Day said. "Every day is like a dream. The Lord has orchestrated a great career."

Whether coming from well off the pace, as he did with Awesome Again (above) in 1998 at Churchill Downs, or nursing a front-runner like Cat Thief (below) in 1999 at Gulfstream Park, Pat Day has been the jockey to beat in the Breeders' Cup Classic. He has proven as versatile and adaptable as the horses he rides.

1999 Breeders' Cup VIP pin.

"The Lord has orchestrated a great career."

Pat Day credits his faith with helping him to accomplish so much both on and off the track. "There's been a tremendous amount of divine intervention throughout my career," he said. "Success begets success, but I believe there is someone orchestrating those opportunities." Raising his helmet to the sky has been a Day trademark since his victory aboard Wild Again in the inaugural Breeders' Cup Classic in 1984 at Hollywood Park. "When I took my helmet off, God was the farthest thing from my mind," he said. "I was just going to kind of pat myself on the back, showboat, but when I reached for my helmet, I was overcome by the voice of God."

Never before had an event come along in racing and immediately been such an unqualified hit. The Breeders' Cup has fostered a new spirit of cooperation in racing, with factions that had gotten along as well as the Hatfields and McCoys finally coming together in the realization that what was good for one was good for all.

There was pressure on the Breeders' Cup in the early years to step beyond its original mission, to become, as D.G. Van Clief, Jr., the president of Breeders' Cup Ltd., puts it, "everything to everybody." But not until the Breeders' Cup was firmly entrenched did it begin to venture far and wide. As racing moves into a new millennium, the Breeders' Cup stands poised at the forefront of the sport, a guiding force taking a prominent leadership role. Most notably, the Breeders' Cup is working closely with the National Thoroughbred Racing Association, racing's national league office, which was created in the late 1990s.

When the NTRA needed start-up funds, the Breeders' Cup came through. The following year, NTRA revenues from stallion seasons came up short, and the Breeders' Cup again stepped up with a donation. In December 1999, the NTRA and Breeders' Cup announced a strategic partnership between the two organizations.

"The future prospects of the Breeders' Cup are tied with the future of the NTRA," Van Clief said. "I look for us to grow closer as we go on. The mission of the Breeders' Cup, although the focus has been much narrower than the NTRA, is that we exist to promote Thoroughbred horse racing and to develop a broad fan base. My personal opinion is that you'll see the two merge at some point in time. The sport's championship should be integrated with the national office, and we should use our resources together.

D.G. Van Clief, Jr.,
President,
Breeders' Cup Ltd.

National Thoroughbred Racing Association pin.

The color and spectacle of Thoroughbred racing comes alive gloriously each year when great horses and great jockeys line up for the Breeders' Cup. The congregation of excellence is unlike anything else in international racing. Royal Ascot outside London is spread over four days. Arc de Triomphe weekend in Paris is spread over two days. For one day, at one track, nothing compares to this extravaganza.

"The Breeders' Cup brings to the NTRA the assets of a racing championship," Van Clief added. "The keystone is our television packages. We can make the NTRA more attractive to sponsors and advertisers. We bring 17 years of industry leadership. We have a good relationship with the industry. We are a fairly focused organization. Part of our mission was to have a viable, network-level property. We're still fairly lean with a narrow focus. We keep our eye on the bullseye of building a championship day of racing, the world's best day of racing, but we're expanding our mission to the broader concept of marketing Thoroughbred racing. The NTRA has a broad marketing outlook, so it's a natural fit. We can go forward with more effectiveness. One plus one equals three."

The Breeders' Cup has come a long way since its conceptualization. It was initially viewed with some skepticism, but that soon changed, and the Breeders' Cup quickly became viewed as a savior. Van Clief believes the

Breeders' Cup grew appropriately, never overextending itself, finally expanding its horizons when it was solidly established.

"There were plenty of doubters at the beginning," Van Clief recalled. "Few people believed the Kentucky breeders could get along, let alone all the breeders, and that they in turn could work with the racetracks. In 1984 and 1985, there was great debate over whether the Breeders' Cup should become the national marketing office for

the sport, or stay narrow, which was the right thing to do at that point. I think if we had tried to be everything to everybody we might not have made it.

"We were the first organization to bring disparate groups together at the national level," Van Clief added. "I think the lasting contribution of the Breeders' Cup in the last century was that it was the first organization to show that this kind of coalition enterprise can work."

The spirit of cooperation fostered by the Breeders' Cup led to the American Championship Racing Series, and then the Champions on FOX Series, races for older horses who might have first become known to the public during the Triple Crown. There is now a rhythm and logic to the season following the Triple Crown. Racing fans, like those of baseball and football, now have compelling story lines they can follow straight through to a climactic, season-ending championship.

"I think we can look back with pride at what we've accomplished," Van Clief said. "We've had an impact on the promotion of the sport, television, and marketing."

But the Breeders' Cup has not, and will not, stand still. The Championship day program originally was worth $10 million. Now, it is $13 million. Originally, there were seven races, but in 1999, the program was expanded to eight, with the Breeders' Cup Filly and Mare Turf. In addition, rules regarding supplemental entries have been refined and improved.

"From the time I came on board, the two questions we were asked most often were, When are you going to have a grass race for fillies and mares, and when are you going to change the rules for supplementary entries?" Van Clief said. "In making the additional million-dollar commitment to the Breeders' Cup Filly and Mare Turf, we had to make sure we could stand on our feet financially to support the race. We think the race will enhance the willingness to nominate fillies on both sides of the Atlantic. We're already seeing an upturn. It's been warmly received."

Adding a pin each year to the hat of Ferguson Taylor of Breeders' Cup Ltd. has become an annual tradition.

SOARING SOFTLY – 1999 Filly & Mare Turf

When owner John Phillips and trainer Jim Toner found out that the Breeders' Cup was going to add a turf race for fillies and mares beginning in 1999, they figured the race would come one year too late. Their mare, Memories of Silver, had been one of the top female turf runners in the late 1990s, but when it came to the Breeders' Cup, she was a square peg in a round hole. She was not good enough to beat the boys, though she did try in the 1996 Breeders' Cup Mile, finishing fifth. With no Breeders' Cup race on the turf exclusively for females, Memories of Silver did not participate again in the Breeders' Cup before being retired in 1998. But fate smiled on Phillips and Toner. They had the best female turf runner of 1999, Soaring Softly, and this time they had a place to showcase her on Breeders' Cup Championship day. When jockey Jerry Bailey brought Soaring Softly back to the winner's circle at Gulfstream Park after the inaugural Breeders' Cup Filly and Mare Turf (inset), it was the perfect ending to the saga of Phillips and Toner, and a great beginning for the Breeders' Cup's newest race.

The Breeders' Cup Filly and Mare Turf had an immediate impact. In its first year, the winner, Soaring Softly, was honored with the Eclipse Award as champion female turf runner.

The Breeders' Cup certainly has changed racing. The sport has become far more international, both in terms of the horses who arrive here to compete—such as European champion Daylami, the dazzling winner of the 1999 Breeders' Cup Turf—and through the aggressive expansion of simulcasting to overseas markets. The schedule of national stakes leading up to the Breeders' Cup has been altered to give horses appropriate prep races. And a horse who can complete his year with a Breeders' Cup victory places himself in prime consideration for championship honors.

For every breeder, the dream begins anew each spring, when each new, adorable foal takes its first wobbly, tentative step minutes after being born. Instinctively, they want to run, and soon they are racing through the fields, giving rise to the hope that one youngster—the precocious one that just flashed by right there—will be the one who becomes a Breeders' Cup champion.

In 1999 at Gulfstream Park (right), both the Breeders' Cup Turf and Breeders' Cup Classic became a part of the Emirates World Series Racing Championship, an ambitious program designed to have the world's greatest horses compete in top-class races all over the globe. Emirates Airlines, based in Dubai in the United Arab Emirates, sponsors the series, and has added an exotic flair (middle) to Breeders' Cup Championship day. A special trophy (bottom) has been created for the series, which was the brainchild of Sheikh Mohammed al Maktoum, a member of the ruling family of Dubai. His Godolphin Racing stable star, Daylami, clinched the first Emirates series with his win in the 1999 Breeders' Cup Turf. As with the Olympics, events such as the Breeders' Cup and the Emirates World Series Racing Championship use sports as a way to expose people to different cultures, and to foster improved relations between countries.

As John Gaines, the founder of the Breeders' Cup, envisioned 20 years ago, the Breeders' Cup has become racing's World Series, its Super Bowl.

"It was an important conceptual accomplishment, and a significant political accomplishment, because the sport had never cooperated before on a joint venture," Gaines said. "The virtue of cooperation was a wholly new experience for the industry. People can now see that by working together, they can create something positive for the sport."

…Breeders' Cup brought about the dawn of a new era in horse racing, one that stressed coordination and cooperation. Attendance and handle at major events like the Triple Crown races are at record levels. Concerted advertising and promotion has led to greater recognition of the sport. For those who breed horses, those who buy them at auction, and those who race them, the opportunity for financial gain never has been better. The Breeders' Cup, like the Triple Crown races, rewards excellence, and gives horsemen additional incentive to maintain high standards in the breeding, raising, and care of their animals.

Rare is the concept that, once enacted, proves a glorious success. There were great struggles along the way, and there figure to be challenges in the future. But the Breeders' Cup not only has fulfilled its goal of determining how racing's champions are evaluated and chosen, it has changed, for the better, the face of racing.

Appendix

LEADING BREEDERS' CUP CHAMPIONSHIP OWNERS — MONEY WON

NAME	STARTERS	1ST	2ND	3RD	4TH	5TH	6TH	MONEY WON
Allen E. Paulson	32	6	2	7	2	1	1	$7,570,000
Daniel Wildenstein	19	2	4	1	2	1	1	3,917,000
Overbrook Farm (W.T. Young)	22	3	1	4	0	3	0	3,915,000
Ogden Phipps	19	3	5	1	1	0	3	3,611,000
Frank H. Stronach	14	1	0	1	2	3	2	3,488,000
Sheikh Mohammed al Maktoum	19	2	1	4	4	0	1	3,410,000
Frances A. Genter	8	2	3	1	0	0	0	2,835,000
Eugene V. Klein	17	4	3	1	0	0	1	2,593,000
Sam-Son Farms	14	2	1	2	1	1	2	2,382,000
Carolyn Hine	2	1	0	0	0	0	1	2,288,000

LEADING BREEDERS' CUP CHAMPIONSHIP TRAINERS — MONEY WON

NAME	STARTERS	1ST	2ND	3RD	4TH	5TH	6TH	MONEY WON
D. Wayne Lukas	126	15	18	14	7	11	12	$15,836,000
William I. Mott	31	5	6	4	2	1	1	8,382,000
Claude R. McGaughey III	43	7	8	1	5	3	3	6,601,400
Andre Fabre	30	2	4	5	1	2	1	5,405,000
Neil Drysdale	20	5	3	1	3	4	2	5,003,600
Charles Whittingham	24	2	2	3	2	2	2	4,298,000
Patrick Byrne	6	3	0	0	0	0	0	3,718,000
Jack Van Berg	14	1	3	3	1	0	2	3,600,000
Robert Frankel	34	0	4	5	6	1	3	3,279,000
Ronald McAnally	26	4	2	2	2	1	4	3,276,000

LEADING BREEDERS' CUP CHAMPIONSHIP JOCKEYS — MONEY WON

NAME	STARTERS	1ST	2ND	3RD	4TH	5TH	6TH	MONEY WON
Pat Day	89	11	14	10	5	8	8	$19,853,000
Chris McCarron	89	7	11	7	6	6	11	12,760,000
Gary Stevens	76	7	14	9	4	7	7	12,030,680
Jerry Bailey	59	9	5	6	3	6	3	11,775,400
Mike Smith	39	8	3	3	1	5	2	7,860,200
Eddie Delahoussaye	64	7	3	6	8	8	6	7,719,000
Laffit Pincay, Jr.	61	7	4	9	5	3	6	6,811,000
Angel Cordero, Jr.	48	4	7	7	1	6	8	6,020,000
Corey Nakatani	35	5	5	5	3	3	3	5,916,520
Jose Santos	48	6	2	4	6	6	2	5,801,000

Twilight Ridge - 1985

Fly So Free - 1990

BREEDERS' CUP JUVENILE FILLIES

YEAR/TRACK DATE/DISTANCE	WINNER/ OWNER	JOCKEY/ TRAINER	SECOND/ JOCKEY	THIRD/ JOCKEY	TIME/ODDS
1999 - GP Nov. 6 - 1 1/16M	Cash Run Padua Stables	J. Bailey D. W. Lukas	Chilukki D. Flores	Surfside P. Day	1:43.31 $32.50
1998 - CD Nov. 7 - 1 1/16M	Silverbulletday M. Pegram	G. Stevens B. Baffert	Excellent Meeting K. Desormeaux	Three Ring J. Velazquez	1:43.68 $.80
1997 - HOL Nov. 8 - 1 1/16M	Countess Diana Kaster & Propson	S. Sellers P. Byrne	Career Collection C. Nakatani	Primaly M. Smith	1:42.11 $2.00
1996 - WO Oct. 26 - 1 1/16M	Storm Song Dogwood Stable	C. Perret N. Zito	Love That Jazz M. Smith	Critical Factor A. Solis	1:43.60 $1.60
1995 - BEL Oct.28 - 1 1/16 M	My Flag O. Phipps	J. Bailey C. McGaughey III	Cara Rafaela P. Day	Golden Attraction G. Stevens	1:42.55 $3.50
1994- CD Nov. 5- 1 1/16M	Flanders Overbrook Farm	P. Day D. W. Lukas	Serena's Song C. Nakatani	Stormy Blues J. Santos	1:45.28 $.40
1993- SA Nov. 6 - 1 1/16M	Phone Chatter H. Sarkowsky	L. Pincay, Jr. R. Mandella	Sardula E. Delahoussaye	Heavenly Prize M. Smith	1:43.08 $2.30
1992- GP Oct. 31- 1 1/16M	Eliza A. Paulson	P. Valenzuela A. Hassinger, Jr.	Educated Risk J. Bailey	Boots 'n Jackie M. Lee	1:42.93 $1.20
1991- CD Nov.2- 1 1/16M	Pleasant Stage Buckland Farm	E. Delahoussaye C. Speckert	La Spia A. Solis	Cadillac Women P. Compton	1:46.48 $5.80
1990- BEL Oct.27- 1 1/16M	Meadow Star C. Icahn	J. Santos L. Jolley	Private Treasure J. Bailey	Dance Smartly S. Hawley	1:44.00 $.20
1989- GP Nov.4- 1 1/16M	Go for Wand Christiana Stable	R. Romero W. Badgett, Jr.	Sweet Roberta P. Day	Stella Madrid A. Cordero, Jr.	1:44 1/5 $2.50
1988- CD Nov. 5- 1 1/16M	Open Mind E. Klein	A. Cordero, Jr. D. W. Lukas	Darby Shuffle J. Krone	Lea Lucinda L. Pincay, Jr.	1:46 3/5 e-$.70
1987- HOL Nov.21- 1 M	Epitome J. Bell	P. Day P. Hauswald	Jeanne Jones W. Shoemaker	Dream Team C. McCarron	1:36 2/5 $30.40
1986- SA Nov. 1- 1 1/16M	Brave Raj D. Green	P. Valenzuela M. Stute	Tappiano J. Cruguet	Saros Brig W. Shoemaker	1:43 1/5 $4.00
1985- AQU Nov.2- 1M	Twilight Ridge E. Klein	J. Velasquez D. W. Lukas	Family Style L. Pincay, Jr.	Steal A Kiss A. Cordero, Jr.	1:35 4/5 e-$.60
1984- HOL Nov. 10- 1 M	Outstandingly* Harbor View Farm	W. Guerra F. Martin	Dusty Heart D. McHargue	Fine Spirit C. McCarron	1:37 4/5 $22.80

* Placed 1st through disqualification of Fran's Valentine, who was placed 10th.

BREEDERS' CUP JUVENILE

YEAR/TRACK DATE/DISTANCE	WINNER/ OWNER	JOCKEY/ TRAINER	SECOND/ JOCKEY	THIRD/ JOCKEY	TIME/ODDS
1999 - GP Nov. 6 - 1 1/16M	Anees The Thoroughbred Corp.	G. Stevens A. Hassinger, Jr.	Chief Seattle E. Prado	High Yield J. Bailey	1:42.29 $30.30
1998 - CD Nov. 7 - 1 1/16M	Answer Lively J. Franks	J. Bailey B. Barnett	Aly's Alley E. Prado	Cat Thief P. Day	1:44.00 $2.70
1997 - HOL Nov. 8 - 1 1/16M	Favorite Trick J. LaCombe	P. Day P. Byrne	Dawson's Legacy T. Kabel	Nationalore E. Delahoussaye	1:41.47 $1.20
1996 - WO Oct. 26 - 1 1/16M	Boston Harbor Overbrook Farm	J. Bailey D. W. Lukas	Acceptable S. Sellers	Ordway J. Velazquez	1:43.40 $2.40
1995 - BEL Oct.28- 1 1/16 M	Unbridled's Song Paraneck Stable	M. Smith J. Ryerson	Hennessy D. Barton	Editor's Note J. Bailey	1:41.60 $5.20
1994- CD Nov. 5- 1 1/16M	Timber Country Gainesway & Overbrook	P. Day D. W. Lukas	Eltish P. Eddery	Tejano Run J. Bailey	1:44.55 $2.40
1993- SA Nov. 6 - 1 1/16M	Brocco Mr. & Mrs. A. Broccoli	G. Stevens R. Winick	Blumin Affair J. Bailey	Tabasco Cat P. Day	1:42.99 $3.00
1992- GP Oct. 31- 1 1/16M	Gilded Time Milch & Silverman	C. McCarron D. Vienna	It'sali'lknownfact L. Pincay, Jr.	River Special K. Desormeaux	1:43.43 $2.00
1991- CD Nov.2- 1 1/16M	Arazi A. Paulson	P. Valenzuela F. Boutin	Bertrando A. Solis	Snappy Landing G. Stevens	1:44.78 $2.10
1990- BEL Oct.27- 1 1/16M	Fly So Free T. Valando	J. Santos F. Schulhofer	Take Me Out M. Smith	Lost Mountain C. McCarron	1:43 2/5 $1.40
1989- GP Nov.4- 1 1/16M	Rhythm O. M. Phipps	C. Perret C. McGaughey III	Grand Canyon C. McCarron	Slavic J. Santos	1:43 3/5 e-$2.60
1988- CD Nov. 5- 1 1/16M	Is It True E. Klein	L. Pincay, Jr. D. W. Lukas	Easy Goer P. Day	Tagel F. Head	1:46 3/5 $9.20
1987- HOL Nov.21- 1 M	Success Express E. Klein	J. Santos D. W. Lukas	Regal Classic D. Penna	Tejano L. Pincay, Jr.	1:35 1/5 e-$4.10
1986- SA Nov. 1- 1 1/16M	Capote Beal, French Jr. & Klein	L. Pincay, Jr. D. W. Lukas	Qualify G. Stevens	Alysheba W. Shoemaker	1:43 4/5 $2.40
1985- AQU Nov.2- 1M	Tasso G. Robins	L. Pincay, Jr. N. Drysdale	Storm Cat C. McCarron	Scat Dancer S. Soto	1:36 1/5 $5.60
1984- HOL Nov. 10- 1 M	Chief's Crown Star Crown Stable	D. MacBeth R. Laurin	Tank's Prospect J. Velasquez	Spend A Buck A. Cordero, Jr.	1:36 1/5 $.70

BREEDERS' CUP SPRINT

YEAR/TRACK DATE/DISTANCE	WINNER/ OWNER	JOCKEY/ TRAINER	SECOND/ JOCKEY	THIRD/ JOCKEY	TIME/ODDS
1999 - GP Nov. 6 - 6F	Artax Paraneck Stable	J. Chavez L. Albertrani	Kona Gold A. Solis	Big Jag J. Valdivia, Jr.	1:07.89 $3.70
1998 - CD Nov. 7 - 6 F	Reraise Fey, Han, et al.	C. Nakatani C. Dollase	Grand Slam G. Stevens	Kona Gold A. Solis	1:09.07 $3.80
1997 - HOL Nov. 8 - 6 F	Elmhurst Evergreen Farm & Sahadi	C. Nakatani J. Sahadi	Hesabull G. Stevens	Bet On Sunshine P. Day	1:08.01 $16.60
1996 - WO Oct. 26 - 6 F	Lit De Justice Evergreen Farm	C. Nakatani J. Sahadi	Paying Dues P. Day	Honour and Glory G. Stevens	1:08.60 $4.00
1995 - BEL Oct.28 - 6 F	Desert Stormer J. Nor	K. Desormeaux F. Lyons	Mr. Greeley J. Krone	Lit De Justice C. Nakatani	1:09.14 $14.50
1994 - CD Nov. 5 - 6 F	Cherokee Run J. Robinson	M. Smith F. Alexander	Soviet Problem C. McCarron	Cardmania E. Delahoussaye	1:09.54 $2.80
1993 - SA Nov. 6 - 6 F	Cardmania J. Couvercelle	E. Delahoussaye D. Meredith	Meafara G. Stevens	Gilded Time C. McCarron	1:08.76 $5.30
1992 - GP Oct. 31 - 6 F	Thirty Slews DeGroot & DutchMasters III	E. Delahoussaye B. Baffert	Meafara J. Velasquez	Rubiano J. Krone	1:08.21 $18.70
1991 - CD Nov.2 - 6 F	Sheikh Albadou (GB) H. Salem	P. Eddery A. Scott	Pleasant Tap E. Delahoussaye	Robyn Dancer L. Pincay, Jr.	1:09.36 $26.30
1990 - BEL Oct.27 - 6 F	Safely Kept Jayeff B Stable	C. Perret A. Goldberg	Dayjur W. Carson	Black Tie Affair (Ire) L. Pincay, Jr.	1:09 3/5 $12.20
1989 - GP Nov.4 - 6 F	Dancing Spree O. Phipps	A. Cordero, Jr. C. McGaughey III	Safely Kept C. Perret	Dispersal C. McCarron	1:09 $16.60
1988 - CD Nov. 5 - 6 F	Gulch P. Brant	A. Cordero, Jr. D. W. Lukas	Play The King D. Seymour	Afleet G. Stahlbaum	1:10 2/5 e-$5.80
1987 - HOL Nov.21 - 6 F	Very Subtle B. Rochelle	P. Valezuela M. Stute	Groovy A. Cordero, Jr.	Exclusive Enough P. Day	1:08 4/5 $16.40
1986 - SA Nov. 1 - 6 F	Smile Frances Genter Stable	J. Vasquez F. Schulhofer	Pine Tree Lane A. Cordero, Jr.	Bedside Promise L. Pincay, Jr.	1:08 2/5 $11.00
1985 - AQU Nov.2 - 6 F	Precisionist F. Hooper	C. McCarron L. Fenstermaker	Smile J. Vasquez	Mt. Livermore J. Velasquez	1:08 2/5 $3.40
1984 - HOL Nov. 10 - 6 F	Eillo Crown Stable	C. Perret B. Lepman	Commemorate C. McCarron	Fighting Fit E. Delahoussaye	1:10 1/5 $1.30

BREEDERS' CUP MILE

YEAR/TRACK DATE/DISTANCE	WINNER/ OWNER	JOCKEY/ TRAINER	SECOND/ JOCKEY	THIRD/ JOCKEY	TIME/ODDS
1999 - GP Nov. 6 - 1M(T)	Silic (Fr) Lanni, Schiappa, Poslosky	C. Nakatani J. Canani	Tuzla (Fr) D. Flores	Docksider G. Stevens	1:34.26 $7.20
1998 - CD Nov. 7 - 1 M(T)	Da Hoss Prestonwood Farm, et al.	J. Velazquez M. Dickinson	Hawksley Hill (Ire) A. Solis	Labeeb (GB) K. Desormeaux	1:35.27 $11.60
1997 - HOL Nov. 8 - 1 M(T)	Spinning World Flaxman Holdings Ltd	C. Asmussen J. Pease	Geri J. Bailey	Decorated Hero (GB) L. Dettori	1:32.77 $2.10
1996 - WO Oct. 26 - 1 M(T)	Da Hoss Prestonwood Farm	G. Stevens M. Dickinson	Spinning World C. Asmussen	Same Old Wish S. Sellers	1:35.80 $8.45
1995 - BEL Oct.28 - 1 M(T)	Ridgewood Pearl (Ire) A. Coughlan	J. Murtagh J. Oxx	Fastness (Ire) G. Stevens	Sayyedati (GB) C. Nakatani	1:43.65 $2.55
1994 - CD Nov. 5 - 1 M(T)	Barathea (Ire) M. al Maktoum & Leigh	L. Dettori L. Cumani	Johann Quatz (Fr) A. Solis	Unfinished Symph G. Baze	1:34.50 $10.40
1993 - SA Nov. 6 - 1 M(T)	Lure Claiborne & Gamely Corp.	M. Smith C. McGaughey III	Ski Paradise T. Jarnet	Fourstars Allstar J. Santos	1:33.58 $1.30
1992 - GP Oct. 31 - 1 M(T)	Lure Claiborne Farm	M. Smith C. McGaughey III	Paradise Creek P. Day	Brief Truce M. Kinane	1:32.90 $5.40
1991 - CD Nov.2 - 1 M(T)	Opening Verse A. Paulson	P. Valenzuela R. Lundy	Val des Bois (Fr) C. McCarron	Star of Cozzene P. Day	1:37.59 $26.70
1990 - BEL Oct.27 - 1 M(T)	Royal Academy Classic Ire Stable	L. Piggott V. O'Brien	Itsallgreektome C. Nakatani	Priolo C. Asmussen	1:35 1/5 $2.80
1989 - GP Nov.4 - 1 M(T)	Steinlen (GB) Wildenstein Stable	J. Santos D. W. Lukas	Sabona C. McCarron	Most Welcome G. Carter	1:37 1/5 $1.80
1988 - CD Nov. 5 - 1 M(T)	Miesque S. Niarchos	F. Head F. Boutin	Steinlen (GB) L. Pincay, Jr.	Simply Majestic A. Cordero, Jr.	1:38 3/5 e-$2.00
1987 - HOL Nov.21 - 1 M(T)	Miesque S. Niarchos	F. Head F. Boutin	Show Dancer M. Castaneda	Sonic Lady L. Pincay, Jr.	1:32 4/5 $3.60
1986 - SA Nov. 1 - 1 M(T)	Last Tycoon (Ire) R. Strauss	Y. Saint-Martin R. Collet	Palace Music G. Stevens	Fred Astaire R. Romero	1:35 1/5 $35.90
1985 - AQU Nov.2 - 1 M(T)	Cozzene J. Nerud	W. Guerra J. Nerud	Al Mamoon* A. Cordero, Jr.	Shadeed W. Swinburn	1:35 $3.60
1984 - HOL Nov. 10 - 1 M(T)	Royal Heroine (Ire) R. Sangster	F. Toro J. Gosden	Star Choice J. McKnight	Cozzene W. Guerra	1:32 3/5 e-$1.70

* Placed 2nd through disqualification of Palace Music, who was placed 9th.

Artax - 1999

Lure - 1992

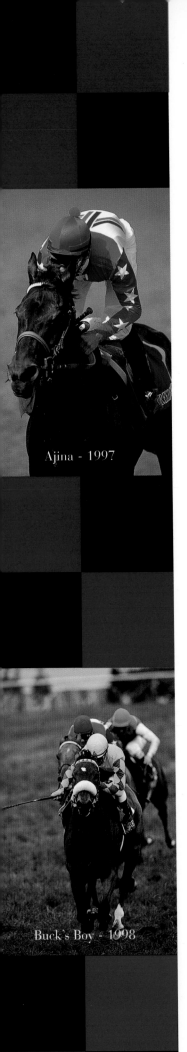

Ajina - 1997

Buck's Boy - 1998

BREEDERS' CUP DISTAFF

YEAR/TRACK DATE/DISTANCE	WINNER/ OWNER	JOCKEY/ TRAINER	SECOND/ JOCKEY	THIRD/ JOCKEY	TIME/ODDS
1999 - GP Nov. 6 - 1 1/8M	**Beautiful Pleasure** J. Oxley	J. Chavez J. Ward, Jr.	**Banshee Breeze** P. Day	Heritage of Gold S. Sellers	1:47.56 $3.00
1998 - CD Nov. 7 - 1 1/8M	**Escena** A. Paulson	G. Stevens W. Mott	**Banshee Breeze** J. Bailey	Keeper Hill C. McCarron	1:49.89 $3.00
1997 - HOL Nov. 8 - 1 1/8M	**Ajina** A. Paulson	M. Smith W. Mott	**Sharp Cat** A. Solis	Escena J. Bailey	1:47.20 $4.80
1996 - WO Oct. 26 - 1 1/8M	**Jewel Princess** Stephen & The Thoroughbred Corp.	C. Nakatani W. Dollase	**Serena's Song** G. Stevens	Different (Arg) C. McCarron	1:48.40 $2.40
1995 - BEL Oct.28 - 1 1/8 M	**Inside Information** O. M. Phipps	M. Smith C. McGaughey	**Heavenly Prize** P. Day	Lakeway K. Desormeaux	1:46.15 $.80
1994- CD Nov. 5 - 1 1/8M	**One Dreamer** Glen Hill Farm	G. Stevens T. Proctor	**Heavenly Prize** P. Day	Miss Dominique C. Nakatani	1:50.70 $47.10
1993- SA Nov. 6 - 1 1/8 M	**Hollywood Wildcat** I. & M. Cowan	E. Delahoussaye N. Drysdale	**Paseana (Arg)** C. McCarron	Re Toss (Arg) C. Nakatani	1:48.35 $1.30
1992- GP Oct. 31- 1 1/8 M	**Paseana (Arg)** S. Craig	C. McCarron R. McAnally	**Versailles Treaty** M. Smith	Magical Maiden G. Stevens	1:48.17 $2.70
1991- CD Nov.2- 1 1/8M	**Dance Smartly** Sam-Son Farm	P. Day J. Day	**Versailles Treaty** A. Cordero, Jr.	Brought To Mind P. Valenzuela	1:50.95 $.50
1990- BEL Oct.27- 1 1/8M	**Bayakoa (Arg)** F. Whitham	L. Pincay, Jr. R. McAnally	**Colonial Waters** J. Santos	Valay Maid M. Castaneda	1:49 1/5 $1.10
1989- GP Nov.4- 1 1/8M	**Bayakoa (Arg)** F. Whitham	L. Pincay, Jr. R. McAnally	**Gorgeous** E. Delahoussaye	Open Mind A. Cordero, Jr.	1:47 2/5 $.70
1988- CD Nov. 5- 1 1/8M	**Personal Ensign** O. Phipps	R. Romero C. McGaughey III	**Winning Colors** G. Stevens	Goodbye Halo E. Delahoussaye	1:52 $.50
1987- HOL Nov.21- 1 1/4M	**Sacahuista** Beal & French Jr.	R. Romero D. W. Lukas	**Clabber Girl** L. Pincay, Jr.	Oueee Bebe E. Delahoussaye	2:02 4/5 $2.90
1986- SA Nov. 1- 1 1/4M	**Lady's Secret** Mr. & Mrs. E.V. Klein	P. Day D. W. Lukas	**Fran's Valentine** W. Shoemaker	Outstandingly G. Stevens	2:01 1/5 $.50
1985- AQU Nov.2- 1 1/4M	**Life's Magic** M. Hatley & E. Klein	A. Cordero, Jr. D. W. Lukas	**Lady's Secret** J. Velasquez	DontstopThemusic L. Pincay, Jr.	2:02 e- $.40
1984- HOL Nov. 10- 1 1/4 M	**Princess Rooney** P. Tucker	E. Delahoussaye N. Drysdale	**Life's Magic** J. Velasquez	Adored L. Pincay, Jr.	2:02 2/5 $.70

BREEDERS' CUP TURF

YEAR/TRACK DATE/DISTANCE	WINNER/ OWNER	JOCKEY/ TRAINER	SECOND/ JOCKEY	THIRD/ JOCKEY	TIME/ODDS
1999 - GP Nov. 6 - 1 1/2M(T)	**Daylami (Ire)** Godolphin Racing Inc.	L. Dettori S. bin Suroor	**Royal Anthem** G. Stevens	Buck's Boy G. Gomez	2:24.73 $1.60
1998 - CD Nov. 7 - 1 1/2M(T)	**Buck's Boy** Quarter B. Farm	S. Sellers N. Hickey	**Yagli** C. Nakatani	Dushyantor K. Desormeaux	2:28.74 $3.60
1997 - HOL Nov. 8 - 1 1/2M(T)	**Chief Bearhart** Sam-Son Farm	J. Santos M. Frostad	**Borgia (Ger)** K. Fallon	Flag Down J. Bailey	2:23.92 $1.90
1996 - WO Oct. 26 - 1 1/2M(T)	**Pilsudski (Ire)** Lord Weinstock	W. Swinburn M. Stoute	**Singspiel (Ire)** G. Stevens	Swain (Ire) O. Peslier	2:30.20 $13.70
1995 - BEL Oct.28- 1 1/2 M(T)	**Northern Spur (Ire)** C. Cella	C. McCarron R. McAnally	**Freedom Cry (GB)** O. Peslier	Carnegie (Ire) T. Jarnet	2:42.07 $3.95
1994- CD Nov. 5- 1 1/2M(T)	**Tikkanen** Augustin Stable	M. Smith J. Pease	**Hatoof** W. Swinburn	Paradise Creek P. Day	2:26.50 $16.60
1993- SA Nov. 6 - 1 1/2 M(T)	**Kotashaan (Fr)** La Presle Farm	K. Desormeaux R. Mandella	**Bien Bien** C. McCarron	Luazur (Fr) P. Day	2:25.16 $1.50
1992- GP Oct. 31- 1 1/2 M(T)	**Fraise** M. Paulson	P. Valenzuela W. Mott	**Sky Classic** P. Day	Quest For Fame (GB) P. Eddery	2:24.08 $14.00
1991- CD Nov.2- 1 1/2M(T)	**Miss Alleged** Fares Farm Inc.	E. Legrix B. Pascal	**Itsallgreektome** J. Velasquez	Quest For Fame (GB) P. Eddery	2:30.95 $42.10
1990- BEL Oct.27- 1 1/2M(T)	**In The Wings (GB)** Mohammed Al Maktoum	G. Stevens A. Fabre	**With Approval** C. Perret	El Senor A. Cordero, Jr.	2:29 3/5 $1.90
1989- GP Nov.4- 1 1/2M(T)	**Prized** Clover Stables, et al.	E. Delahoussaye N. Drysdale	**Sierra Roberta (Fr)** P. Eddery	Star Lift (GB) G. Stevens	2:28 $8.80
1988- CD Nov. 5- 1 1/2M(T)	**Great Communicator** Class Act Stable	R. Sibille T. Ackel	**Sunshine Forever** A. Cordero, Jr.	Indian Skimmer M. Roberts	2:35 1/5 $12.40
1987- HOL Nov.21- 1 1/2M(T)	**Theatrical** A. Paulson	P. Day W. Mott	**Trempolino** P. Eddery	Village Star (Fr) C. Asmussen	2:24 2/5 $1.80
1986- SA Nov. 1- 1 1/2M(T)	**Manila** B. Shannon	J. Santos L. Jolley	**Theatrical** G. Stevens	Estrapade F. Toro	2:25 2/5 $8.80
1985- AQU Nov.2- 1 1/2M(T)	**Pebbles (GB)** Mohammed Al Maktoum	P. Eddery C. Brittain	**Strawberry Road (Aus)** S. Cauthen	Mourjane (Fr) R. Migliore	2:27 $2.20
1984- HOL Nov.10- 1 1/2 M(T)	**Lashkari (GB)** H. H. Aga Khan	Y. Saint-Martin A. De Royer Dupre	**All Along (Fr)** A. Cordero, Jr.	Raami (GB) F. Toro	2:25 1/5 $53.40

BREEDERS' CUP CLASSIC

YEAR/TRACK DATE/DISTANCE	WINNER/ OWNER	JOCKEY/ TRAINER	SECOND/ JOCKEY	THIRD/ JOCKEY	TIME/ODDS
1999 - GP Nov. 6 - 1 1/4M	**Cat Thief** Overbrook Farm	P. Day D. W. Lukas	**Budroyale** G. Gomez	**Golden Missile** K. Desormeaux	1:59.52 $19.60
1998 - CD Nov. 6 - 1 1/4M	**Awesome Again** F. Stronach Stables	P. Day P. Byrne	**Silver Charm** G. Stevens	**Swain** L. Dettori	2:02.16 $4.70
1997 - HOL Nov. 8 - 1 1/4M	**Skip Away** Carolyn Hine	M. Smith H. Hine	**Deputy Commander** C. Nakatani	**Dowty*** G. Stevens	1:59.16 $1.80
1996 - WO Oct. 26 - 1 1/4M	**Alphabet Soup** Ridder Thoroughbred Stable	C. McCarron D. Hofmans	**Louis Quatorze** P. Day	**Cigar** J. Bailey	2:01.00 $19.85
1995 - BEL Oct. 28 - 1 1/4M	**Cigar** A. Paulson	J. Bailey B. Mott	**L'Carriere** J. Chavez	**Unaccounted For** P. Day	1:59.58 $.70
1994 - CD Nov. 5 - 1 1/4M	**Concern** R. Meyerhoff	J. Bailey R. Small	**Tabasco Cat** P. Day	**Dramatic Gold** C. Nakatani	2:02.41 $7.50
1993 - SA Nov. 6 - 1 1/4M	**Arcangues** D. Wildenstein	J. Bailey A. Fabre	**Bertrando** G. Stevens	**Kissin Kris** P. Day	2:00.83 $133.60
1992 - GP Oct. 31 - 1 1/4M	**A.P. Indy** Farish, Goodman, et al	E. Delahoussaye N. Drysdale	**Pleasant Tap** G. Stevens	**Jolypha** P. Eddery	2:00.20 $2.10
1991 - CD Nov. 2 - 1 1/4M	**Black Tie Affair (Ire)** J. Sullivan	J. Bailey E. Poulos	**Twilight Agenda** C. McCarron	**Unbridled** C. Perret	2:02.95 $4.00
1990 - BEL Oct. 27- 1 1/4M	**Unbridled** F. Genter	P. Day C. Nafzger	**Ibn Bey (GB)** T. Quinn	**Thirty Six Red** M. Smith	2:02 1/5 e-$6.60
1989 - GP Nov. 4 - 1 1/4M	**Sunday Silence** Gaillard, Hancock et al	C. McCarron C. Whittingham	**Easy Goer** P. Day	**Blushing John** A. Cordero, Jr.	2:00 1/5 $2.00
1988 - CD Nov. 5 - 1 1/4M	**Alysheba** D. & P. Scharbauer	C. McCarron J. Van Berg	**Seeking the Gold** P. Day	**Waquoit** J. Santos	2:04 4/5 $1.50
1987 - HOL Nov. 21 - 1 1/4M	**Ferdinand** Mrs. H. Keck	B. Shoemaker C. Whittingham	**Alysheba** C. McCarron	**Judge Angelucci** E. Delahoussaye	2:01 2/5 $1.00
1986 - SA Nov. 1 - 1 1/4M	**Skywalker** Oak Cliff Stable	L. Pincay, Jr. M. Whittingham	**Turkoman** P. Day	**Precisionist** G. Stevens	2:00 2/5 $10.10
1985 - AQU Nov. 2 - 1 1/4M	**Proud Truth** Darby Dan Farm	J. Velasquez J. Veitch	**Gate Dancer** C. McCarron	**Turkoman** J. Vasquez	2:00 4/5 $7.40
1984 - HOL Nov. 10 - 1 1/4M	**Wild Again** Black Chip Stable	P. Day V. Timphony	**Slew O' Gold**** A. Cordero, Jr.	**Gate Dancer** L. Pincay, Jr.	2:03 2/5 $31.30

* Placed 3rd through disqualification of Whiskey Wisdom, who was placed 4th.
** Placed 2nd through disqualification of Gate Dancer, who was placed 3rd.

BREEDERS' CUP FILLY & MARE TURF

YEAR/TRACK DATE/DISTANCE	WINNER/ OWNER	JOCKEY/ TRAINER	SECOND/ JOCKEY	THIRD/ JOCKEY	TIME/ODDS
1999 - GP Nov. 6 - 1 3/8M	**Soaring Softly** Phillips Racing Partnership	J. Bailey J. Toner	**Coretta (Ire)** J. Santos	**Zomaradah (GB)** L. Dettori	2:13.89 $3.60

Skywalker - 1986

Index of Winners

Breeders' Cup Limited gives very special thanks and acknowledgement to the many wonderful photographers who have worked on the Breeders' Cup team in the past 17 years, without whom this book would not be possible, especially Dan Dry & Associates, whose team over the years consisted of Todd Anderson, Mark Ashman, Gary Bogden, Todd Buchanan, Dave Coyle, Gretchen Davis, Jeff Dodge, Steve Dowell, Dan Dry, Margaret Dry, Weasie Gaines, Jim Gensheimer, Jebb Harris, Greg Lovett, Brad Mangin, Gary Mook, Joe Patronite, Rick

Rickman, David Robertson, Patrick Schneider, Thom Shelby, Marty Snortum, Ben Van Hook, Joe Vitti and Scott Wiseman; and JaneArt Limited, whose team consisted of Art Klonsky, Victah Sailer, Eric Schweikhardt, Jane Sobel and Bruce Wodder. Also Brant Gamma, Dell Hancock, Tony Leonard and Bill Straus.

Moonlight Press wishes to thank Katey Barret, Barbara Livingston, Preston Mack, Shig Kikkawa, Kinetic Corporation, Geoff Carr, and Bob Coglianese for their valued contributions.